THE CHANGING PATTERN OF
INTERNATIONAL ECONOMIC AFFAIRS

The Changing Pattern of International Economic Affairs

by

HERBERT FEIS

"defense . . . is of much more importance than opulence . . ."
—ADAM SMITH

HARPER & BROTHERS PUBLISHERS

NEW YORK AND LONDON

1940

THE CHANGING PATTERN OF
INTERNATIONAL ECONOMIC AFFAIRS

FIRST EDITION

K-P

To

R. S-B. F.

CONTENTS

PREFACE

If thoughts, like flowers, grew in beds, it could be said that up until recent years almost all thought upon international economic relations grew in a neatly planted and attractive bed. The seeds had been planted long ago by the great economists of the classical tradition. Hume, Adam Smith, Ricardo, John Stuart Mill, Alfred Marshall, Frank W. Taussig, were among the great gardeners. This bed had a fine pattern and order, and to the sunny intellect, glowing colors. It made the world a pleasant place to live in.

It now lies trampled as though a tank had passed over it. The emergence of great states combining in their national effort a spirit of economic revolt and of military aggressiveness, the disturbances and antagonisms that preceded the war, and now the war itself—all these have thrown into great confusion and uncertainty all economic relations, and all thought as to their future character.

I share the sense of confusion and uncertainty. I welcomed all the more, therefore, the invitation of Columbia University to deliver a short series of lectures in this field as an opportunity to clarify, for myself, and it is hoped for others, both the past and present basis and character of international economic relations. The result is a rather comprehensive and discursive essay.

The course of events has thrust out of the area of

immediate interest or importance many of the technical refinements and intricacies to which most attention is frequently devoted in treatments of the subject. Try, also, as I might to concentrate the analysis on economic affairs, it proved essential at every turn of thought to take reckoning of the state of political and social affairs. In fact, I think that the main shortcoming of the great literature of the past to which I have referred is that it took these matters too little into account in shaping its reasoning. Hence, in any other political and social environment except that which was tacitly assumed, the reasoning all too often has a character of abstract argument.

In these lectures I was on holiday from my official post. The judgments or opinions which are set forth should in no way be taken as expressive of the State Department's policy in any matter touched upon. In print it is much easier to be certain and unfailingly logical than it is in the daily interplay of actual events as they present themselves on the desk of any government official.

I wish to express my sincere thanks for the help given me by Mr. Leroy Stinebower in the preparation of the manuscript, and my friend Dr. Benjamin B. Wallace of the United States Tariff Commission for his critical reading of it. I am appreciative, also, of the obliging consent of Prof. Horace Taylor of Columbia University, which made possible this publication of the lectures.

HERBERT FEIS

THE CHANGING PATTERN OF
INTERNATIONAL ECONOMIC AFFAIRS

I

THE PATTERN FOR WHICH REASON REACHED

THE PLEASING CONCEPTION OF HARMONY

ONE hot summer night the young composer, George Gershwin, was sitting with a friend on the boardwalk of a crowded beach resort near New York City. The night about them was loud with explosive sound. A million human voices rose in talk, in shrieks, and in laughter. As the brightly-lit merry-go-round revolved, its clanking tune rose high. The barkers shouted their hoarse invitations. The little cars rushed down the inclines of the scenic railway with the fierce, grinding noise of steel against steel, and the subway cars sent out their deep roar from underground. The waves tumbled heavily upon the beach.

Gershwin turned and said: "All of this could form such a beautiful pattern of sound. It could turn into a magnificent musical piece expressive of every human activity and feeling—with pauses, counterpoints, blends and climaxes of sound that would be beautiful. But it is not that; it never, I suppose, will come out that way. The different sounds clash, dominate and frustrate each other, that everlasting high whine of the merry-go-round, for example, every so often kills all else, the roar of the subway train spreads when some-

—1—

thing else should be heard. It is all discordant, terrible, and exhausting—as we hear it now. The pattern is always being shattered."

Such an endeavor of the senses to grasp a pattern of sound would appear to be wholly different from the reaching out of minds to grasp a pattern of economic relationship. But the impulse and the effort are in fact similar. The economists of the past, whose analyses of international economic relations have won the greatest renown, spent their working lives in an endeavor similar to that of Gershwin's—to find and develop a pattern of harmony amidst the constant din and movement of events. Unlike Gershwin, they came to believe that the pattern existed and they could see it. This pattern of thought is set forth and refined with brilliant detail and illustration in a hundred books which derive their structure, their central ideas, and their purpose from the early works of Hume, Adam Smith, Ricardo, and Mill. It will be found embedded in the mind of almost every economist, trained like myself in the analysis and doctrines which previous generations of writers and students expounded. Thus we lean toward an interpretation of international economic affairs that attributes to them an affirmatively beneficial and unifying character; we lean away from analyses that reflect primarily division and conflict.

The skillfully wrought pattern of inherited thought is a combination of description, analysis, and argument. The description makes up the assumptions on which the whole pattern of reasoning rests. It seemed to emerge, or almost to emerge, directly from observation of international economic activity itself and, during the period of its ascendancy, to be a substantially true report—a clarified and simplified view of reality. The analysis would fain explain how international economic relations tend to work out and how the behavior of each group or nation affects other groups or nations. The argument attempted to demonstrate how great the universal benefit of economic dealings between peoples would be, if governments would permit them to take an unhindered course.

The conclusions of this doctrine were set forth as the lines of policy to be pursued by nations. Its authors were trying to lead the different countries of the world to modify the restrictive national economic policies which, according to their belief, injured all countries and brought recurrent misery and war. The fuller their studies, the clearer the wisdom of this aim seemed to appear. Inspired with this feeling, they carried on their attempts to clarify the principles of international economic relations and to familiarize the world with their conception of international economic order. They offered a prospect of improvement in the conditions of working life everywhere and of peaceful and friendly relations between countries, thus combining in their vision both material improvement and heart's desire.

This pattern of thought regarding international economic affairs was the natural counterpart of the reasoning of the economists about other economic matters. It was an extension beyond national boundaries of those principles of *laissez faire* that they were expounding.[1] Hence what they asked of government was

[1] Thus as expressly stated by Professor F. W. Taussig in the Preface to his inner-reaching study *International Trade* (p. viii): "It is strictly an inquiry on a particular phase of the system of private property and capitalistic enterprise. It assumes that system to exist, for good or ill, and examines merely the way it works."

not so much an active and conscious cooperation, but abstention from acts that would restrict or block private economic activity. Except in moderate measure where the necessity seemed compelling, state intervention in the free private conduct of business between nations seemed, in their judgment, to result in injury to that beneficial pattern which private activity tended to weave.

Such is the presentation you will find if you read those books which shaped the thought of the nineteenth century. Such are the conceptions and arguments you will find in most of the textbooks that might now be assigned for your use. I wish to give you the main essentials of that body of thought.

THE RELATIONSHIPS OF INTERNATIONAL COMMERCE

The main economic activity between peoples of different countries is that of commerce, and the analysis of international trade relations is the basic part of that scheme of thought which I am summarizing. Under conditions of private ownership and enterprise, which were taken for granted, it is the initiative of private individuals, anticipating profit, that leads to trade between nations and determines its course. In every country where they are free to do so, producers and merchants seek out opportunities in the import and export trade, and negotiate their bargains. Producers and merchants of each country acquaint themselves with possible demand in their own countries for goods obtainable elsewhere. They ascertain the cost in their own currencies of these goods, they compute expenses and risks and if then a profit seems in sight, the purchase is effected. Each day hundreds of such transactions take place. Producers maintain sales organizations in foreign countries to take advantage of chances for profitable business. Buyers often maintain representatives in foreign countries on the alert for things which may be bought there and sold for a profit at home. Governments sustain large organizations whose official purpose is to discover and report upon opportunities for export. For many commodities—primarily such important staples as wheat, cotton, rubber and coffee— there exist organized centers of trade where the dealers in these commodities meet to transact business. Reports are published daily on the market prices of many commodities in different parts of the world—in some instances by governments, in some by the organized exchanges, in some by brokers or other middlemen. On the basis of these reports judgments are made as to where possibilities for business exist and orders are transferred from point to point.

Such have been till recently the prevailing methods of conducting international commerce and so they are pictured in the pattern I am describing. The great commercial centers of the world, London and Liverpool, Hamburg and Bremen, Le Havre and Paris, New York and New Orleans, and a hundred other places, all dealt with each other each day to arrange the exchange of goods. Salesmen and buyers engaged in this commerce formed the staple passenger traffic of the railway and steamship lines.

The commerce of each country with the rest of the world, according to the analysis I am presenting, rests on a twofold basis: First, each country bought from abroad goods which it could not itself produce. Take English trade for instance: the great English textile industry required cotton that could not be raised in England; the English drank tea that had to be grown in a warmer clime; they had a taste for oranges that could only be grown where the sun was stronger. Obversely, many other countries lacked coal which lay in such deep veins in England; they needed the woolen cloth which was spun and woven so well in the great damp of England. So with other countries, each is in a position to supply others with some goods that they themselves cannot produce, and each must depend upon the rest for many goods it cannot produce. This is the simplest basis for trade and is generally known as non-competitive trade. No reflection is required to understand how it operated. But it was by no means the whole of and in many instances not even the main part of the international commerce that was transacted.

Each country differed from the rest in resources, economic organization, skill, social arrangements. As a matter of everyday fact, producers and merchants found profitable markets for commodities in countries where these commodities might be produced, or some equally satisfactory substitute commodity might be produced, but at a higher price. International commerce, when unrestricted, brings the producers of every commodity in every country into price comparison with the producers of the same commodity in other countries. It comes about therefore that to the extent to which international commerce is permitted to take its course, and costs of transport are reduced, nations specialize. Production at home of goods which could be more cheaply acquired from abroad is confined to such low-cost domestic producers as may be able to stand the brunt, or is foregone altogether. Capital and enterprise of the country stay out of these branches of production, and occupy themselves in others where they can meet foreign competition. In certain directions, relatively favored in some way either by nature, circumstance, or acquired skill, the capital enterprise and labor of each country prove themselves among the cheap world producers; these become its export industries. Trade between countries takes place, therefore, if it is permitted, not only in goods in which they could not possibly be competitive producers, but also in goods partly or wholly, directly or indirectly, competitive. The goods which each country acquires from abroad are those that it either cannot produce, or could only produce at a most disadvantageous scale of cost, comparatively. The goods which each country sells abroad are either those that other countries cannot produce, or those which it produces on the most advantageous terms, comparatively.

This became known as the rule of greatest comparative advantage.[2] It was set forth as an explanation of how, if commerce is left free, the international division of labor and production is determined.

It was set apart from the analysis of production and exchange *within* individual countries by the fact that labor and capital and social institutions do not freely cross national boundaries. For if there were no marked reluctance on the part of labor and capital to move from one country to another, and no serious government or other obstacles to such movement, the basis of international trade would not be essentially different

[2] I agree with B. B. Wallace's suggestion that the "rule of comparison of relative advantages" would be both a more adequate and more illuminating term.

from that of domestic trade. However, the contrary conditions prevail. Therefore, it was explained, production is carried on under very unequal conditions in different countries and with very different levels of reward to capital and labor. These differences in reward give to international trade some characteristics basically different from those of trade within a country.

It is in *competition* that the analysis finds the force that shaped the movement and distribution of international trade according to the rule of greatest comparative advantage. Competition was counted upon to operate, in the type of economic system which was in mind, both within each country and between countries. Within each country there is competition for the means of production between all those who believe they can put them to a profitable use. By this competition there are established prices for various kinds of labor, for capital for different purposes, and for the natural resources. Thus there is set, at any given moment, a money cost for particular products which determines roughly the price at which they are offered for sale against similar products produced elsewhere. Competition in the international market then determines what products individuals could profitably produce in each country, what products could be imported at lower money price, what products could be exported to other countries. In each country, so the further reasoning runs, the successful bidders will be those who use the means of production along the most advantageous lines, comparatively. Men will labor at, and capital devote itself to, the making of things most effectively within each country. The division of the world's economic activity gives results by which all benefit.

I pass to another part of the exposition. According to this analysis, what is significant for every country is the *total* trade relationship between itself and the whole of the rest of the world, not that between itself and other individual countries. In fact, the analysis contains an affirmation that there is no need for concern over the course of relationship between individual countries. International commerce and finance, again if left free to operate, will tend to bring about a natural equilibrium as between each country and the rest of the world.

Here I must pass over a vast field of technicalities. The basic conception is this: If the payments which a country must make for imported goods (or for other purposes, such as the payment of debts) exceed the funds that become available to it from its own exports (or other transactions) to the rest of the world, a chain of economic changes and adjustments—affecting prices, wages and other costs—will take place, both inside the country and inside other countries. This course of change and adjustment will tend to restore the balance. It will take place differently under different circumstances. Sometimes it will be brought about as a consequence of the movement of gold from country to country; sometimes it will be brought about merely through changes in the purchasing power of different countries; sometimes it will be brought about by modifications in exchange rates. Thus it was concluded that no country need deplore the fact that it bought at any particular time from any other country more or less than it sold to that other country. Therefore, the trade need not be restricted to such purchases and sales between individual pairs of countries as could directly be brought into equal offsetting amount, or directed to achieve that result. To limit international commerce to such "bilateral" possibilities, is, it was argued, to curtail greatly its possible volume and benefit.

Even further the analysis sought to forestall fears centering about the *total* relationship at any one time between a country and *all* others. In the elastic, continuously adjusting economic systems that were visualized, drains of gold or other assets out of a country tended to produce their own corrective. Conversely, a country drawing greatly on others in the form of gold or other assets would, in time, cease to do so. Hence, except as needed to meet sharp emergency, countries could view with equanimity the rise and fall of their payments to each other.

The benefit from the world-wide scale of trade which was visualized extended to the whole circle of peoples that bought and sold. Even the poorest countries—those to whom nature had given little—who were unskilled, or made lazy by the climate, who were badly governed or demoralized by bad government, would find their share; for in such countries money wages would be low, and the price that came to be set upon some of their products would place them in the international market. In fact, since in very poor countries even most urgent wants remain often unsatisfied, trade might help them more vitally than the rich ones. Rich country and poor country, large country and small country, by directing their labor along lines of greatest comparative advantage, each would be in a position for its own use to draw upon the resources and abilities of the world. The Indian in the villages of the Andes could sell his cocoa for tin sheets to roof his house; the poorest coolie in China could have his lamps lit by the oil of Texas and keep the rain off his back with the cotton cloth of Lancashire or Woonsocket; the Baltic sailor could wear wool grown on the plains of Australia and Argentina and eat the fruit of Spain; the steelmaker in Pittsburgh could have the ores of five continents to make his metal stronger, more durable, stainless. The trading world, in this conception, serves all well by providing the means of making life healthier, more comfortable, more secure, and more interesting. And even more important in its ultimate promise it could make work less laborious and more productive. These were the gains the peoples lost completely if they confined their commerce within their national boundaries, and lost in large measure if they confined it to direct bilateral interchange.

All the history of the past, and these thinkers had pondered over it, had been a record of interferences with trade and of the resistance against such interferences by those who saw prospect of gainful trade. It was a struggle that had gone on when the continent of Europe was divided into thousands of small, independent towns or territories, each of which maintained rigid and harsh restrictions on dealings with "foreigners." It was a struggle also recorded as between towns and the surrounding countryside, each to make the other pay more for what it might need. As the areas of government grew larger and provinces succeeded towns and national states succeeded provinces, the same conflict had been waged between the larger units. The rising spirit of nationality made the larger units no less inclined to curb trade with outsiders—especially import trade—than the smaller ones had been. The readiness to despoil weaker countries by force, rather than to trade with them, continued to flourish. The increased costs of war made the accumulation of gold rather than the improvement of economic life the object of national commercial policy. Thus such trade as it permitted was conducted under watch and license and heavy taxes to protect home production and to make the foreign merchant pay. Suppressed and harried, though, trade had grown formidably through all these periods, and began to form that pattern which these eager minds picked up, explored, and expanded.

Here, then, in contrast with the past, was the cornucopia from which each country might draw. Here was the great consideration which these thinkers hoped governments would grasp. Here was the possibility for which, it was hoped, every country would be willing to undergo the necessary adjustments which the operation of the international pattern inevitably involved. For concert of policy was needed if the full benefit was to be reasonably assured.

Here was the comfort for statesmen in which they could lead their peoples along peaceful and contented lines. For if trade would bring the products that grew outside the national boundaries and would distribute them in some measure to all, the main need and purpose of conquest would seem to vanish. Trade, arising when the world was still divided into hundreds of small political districts, had brought out the need and advantage of larger units. Thus there was evoked in the conception of these writers the idea of a greater unity—that of all the nations of the world in peaceful, economic intercourse. Though some of the notable studies in the field were written during times of bitter and prolonged war, their thought was of peacetime condition and atmosphere. For the hope was active among students of trade that if trade itself could fully realize its potentialities, it would so improve the condition of men that war would become less likely. One of the anticipated rewards was the creation of bonds of peaceful interest which might prevent men of different countries from going to war with each other. The doctrines they propounded were set before all nations in invitation to lay aside fear, hatred, revenge, and lust for conquest—the enemies of men's fortunes. As expressed by John Stuart Mill:

It is commerce which is rapidly rendering war obsolete, by strengthening and multiplying the personal interests which are in natural opposition to it. And it may be said without exaggeration that the great extent and rapid increase of international trade, in being the principal guarantee of the peace of the world, is the great permanent security for the uninterrupted progress of the ideas, the institutions, and the character of the human race.[3]

The economists, thus, in laying out their pattern, had in mind trade determined by the preferences and activities of peoples at peace and in no fear of each

[3] *Principles of Political Economy,* Book III, Chapter XVII.
This may be contrasted with Schmoller's well-known description of the period of the rise of great national states:
"In all ages history has been wont to treat national power and national wealth as sisters. . . . The temptation to the greater states to use their political power for conflict with their economic competitors, and when they could, for their destruction, was too great for them not to succumb time after time, and either to set international law at naught or twist it to their purposes. Commercial competition, even in times nominally of peace, degenerated into a state of undeclared hostility; it plunged nations into one war after another, and gave all wars a turn in the direction of trade, industry, and colonial gain, such as they never had before or after." *The Mercantile System,* p. 64.

other. In part this may have been because war, or even the constant prospect of war, introduced conditions, motives and forms of national economic organization which did not fit into the economists' calculus. Only as peace prevailed could their reasoning rule. In part it may have been a result of the belief and hope that trade would make war obsolete. Even more it may have been because war did not permeate a nation's entire economy as it now does. Preparation for or the fear of war did not cast such long shadows, and lead governments to supplant in thoroughgoing ways the calculations of the market place by calculations of national safety and national power. Even in the bitter wars of the past, much ordinary life largely went on in usual ways.[4] Such extraordinary interferences as there were with the usual economic calculations and decisions of individuals, were chiefly manifested through the exercise of the taxing and monetary policies of the state. Adam Smith, for all his *laissez-faire* predilections, could unreservedly approve the Navigation Acts because

. . . defense . . . is of much more importance than opulence . . .[5]

without regarding this observation as greatly limiting the validity and the general applicability of his main thesis. But today, when war and the preparation for war are "totalitarian," commanding the whole of the nation and all its resources, Smith's exception has enveloped the whole main pattern.

[4] It will be recalled that the slogan "business as usual" was carried into the war of 1914-18 until its full intensity was revealed.
[5] *Wealth of Nations*, Book IV, Chapter II.

International loans or investments were until the nineteenth century sporadic and often of a dubious character. International lending was a business wherein a few wealthy private banking houses provided stores of golden coins to needy kings and emperors to finance their wars, to enable them to fulfill their political engagements or arrange marriages for their children. Or they were in the nature of highly risky commercial transactions expected to produce a fortune quickly, or to fail completely because of the harshness of nature or the cruelty of enemies.

These conditions changed. Well-organized, permanent foreign investment began to take place as the economists carried their reasoning forward. In the economic doctrine I am putting before you, international capital movements were conceived as having their basis in economic opportunity, securing their recompense from economic achievement, and contributing to the increase of international commerce.

Great differences exist between individual countries in the amount of available capital relative to the available resources and labor. It has long since been observed that in countries where there was a great relative supply of capital, in this sense, the rate of return that capital might obtain, tended to decline. This was attributable to the fact that the additional uses of capital did not as greatly augment the productive result as did first uses. In countries where there was comparative lack of capital, the potential increase in product from its use was greater and the chances of gain similarly greater. This—according to the analysis—was the main basis of the movement of capital across national frontiers, though it was recognized that loans to foreign governments might rest on a wholly different one.

International capital movements, so visualized and interpreted, fitted into the developments on which the economists had focused their attention. Inventions were creating new methods and industries. The means of transportation were being improved. Populations were spreading from the more settled and crowded countries to the less settled and uncrowded ones. Trade was growing and the movement of capital appeared a natural part of this expansion. There seemed to be no end to the tasks that the capital accumulated in the older industrial countries might perform in outside centers of occupation. There were lands to be brought under cultivation, railroads to construct, cities to create, factories to equip, mines to dig. All this it was reckoned would bring into the world increased and improved sources of useful goods. Commerce would bring them from the new sources to the investing lands in return for the products of their more established industries. The new field of capital operation, it was judged, would reward investors and contribute to the enrichment of all countries. This was the way in which capital movements fitted into the economists' scheme of international economic relations.

The further technical analysis largely assimilated capital movements to the exchange of goods. The international loan or investment is carried out as a financial transaction. Groups lend or borrow, or invest, sums of money—of pounds sterling, francs, marks. But to the mind tracing these financial transactions through to their ultimate realization, they resolve themselves usually into a movement of commerce.

This result must come about, the explanation runs, because the money proceeds of any loan can ultimately be used only in the country to the lender. Directly, or sometimes through indirect channels and after long delays, this must result. In many cases, it is directly evident. A loan is made, for instance, in New York for the purchase of machinery made in Philadelphia, for a power plant to be erected, let us say, in Bogotá; in this instance the loan expresses itself directly and immediately in a movement of commerce—the shipment of machinery from the United States to Colombia.

In other instances the process may be indirect. A loan, let us say, is contracted in London to pay the wages of men constructing a new port in Australia. In one way or other—the technical explanations are intricate and somewhat in dispute—it comes about through the mechanism of adjustment of international finance that the transfer of the funds loaned from England to Australia will ultimately be discharged through the operation of English commerce. So too, in reverse fashion, repayments on loans are achieved through movements of trade, and the earnings of capital transferred back to the home of the lender through movements of trade. That is the essential conclusion contained in the doctrine that I am outlining.

But more important than this question of how the making of international loans and repayments of them are effected through commerce seemed the economic results produced by the international movement of capital. Capital moving from the more developed economic countries would, it was reckoned, increase production of desired goods elsewhere in the world. By doing this it would not only increase the wealth of the borrowing countries but add to the volume of future commerce in which all would benefit. Nineteenth-century experience seemed to afford ample support to this expectation. Vast new agricultural areas were made available in the United States, Canada, Australia, Argentina, and elsewhere. Great new supplies of raw materials like rubber and jute, copper and tin, were brought into use. Commercial importance was imparted to countries which before were isolated or living by handwork; for example, Japan was equipped with ports, railways, factories, textile and steel mills, and power plants to become a great trading nation. The international movement of capital created a vast new commerce in iron and steel, in machines and tools, in metals and foodstuffs. The whole was deemed to constitute a satisfactory and upbuilding economic performance.

This nourished economists' judgment that there existed the chance of indefinitely large commercial growth open to the participation of all. Capital could safely proceed to its outlying ventures, creating economic activity and production in the borrowing countries, and yielding a share of the additional product to the lending ones. Occasional losses pointed to the need for caution; occasional failures showed that countries might be unable or unwilling to adjust their economic life in the way required of wise lenders and of conscientious borrowers. Occasional critics argued that oppression of large-scale capital in undeveloped lands outweighed its benefits. The economists were not unaware of such risks, difficulties and criticisms. But these seemed definitely subordinate and the result seemed sufficiently certain. Political antagonisms, wars, rebellions, seemed to be diminishing perils to the investor. The steam train and steam shovel, it was thought, would pay their way in all lands, be welcome there, and justify themselves.

ON THE INTERNATIONAL MONETARY SYSTEM

The international monetary system which figures in the body of thought I am setting forth was one operated primarily by private enterprises and left relatively free from government control. It was constituted by the merchant houses carrying on foreign trade, by specialized concerns dealing in bullion movements or in short-term trade finance, or by branches of the large general banking institutions. Such organizations in different countries had close and constant connections with each other. Many of these customarily maintained balances in various foreign currencies to facilitate such ordinary operations as the exchange of one money for another, the financing of commerce, the purchase, sale and shipment of gold and securities. So well established, in fact, were the chief operations of this type that they were regarded as virtually routine.

The operation of the international monetary system was set forth somewhat as follows: Goods are produced, bought and sold for money. Through the international monetary system, the money of each and every country becomes easily exchanged for the money of all other countries. Whoever may have pounds sterling in his pocket, or to his account, for example, has for all purposes dollars, marks or Chinese coin—if he so wishes.

The operation of the system opened up the whole wide world as market for those with goods to sell; it opened up the warehouses of the whole wide world to those who had the money of any country with which to purchase. This was its chief economic function.

In the operation of the monetary system the economists found the explanation of those equilibrating adjustments in the balance of payments between individual countries and the rest of the world—to which I have already referred. Here I must again pass over many technicalities and only hint at explanations. In this field the fine lines of reasoning become as intricate as the designs upon the ceiling of a Persian mosque. Observing how the *relative* values of different currencies became established over a period of time, observing how gold movements between countries were brought about and the effects of such movements, observing changes in interest rates, in purchasing power, in prices and in costs—that occurred in different countries as they dealt with each other—analytical minds discovered in these matters what they considered basic and reliable tendencies. These they offered as an explanation of the conclusion to which they gave support—that without the intervention of governments the payments of each country to all others tended to be brought into balance with the payments received by that country.

In presenting this analysis the economist assumed that nations would permit the necessary changes to take place, and that the conditions of demand would be ordinary. Then, it was reasoned, no overprolonged drain of gold from any country could take place. Plainly if the ruling conditions were fundamentally different from those assumed, the mechanism would not operate and adjustment would fail.

The extent to which nations can or will endure shifts in their economic relations during any period of time, it may be commented, is limited. Countries with an excess of obligations to meet abroad have usually been willing to suffer the diminution of their gold reserves, not their complete exhaustion; they have been willing to adjust to some decline in their general level of prices and money incomes, but not too severe a decline. Correspondingly, countries to which an excess of payments is due have usually been willing to increase somewhat their purchases of foreign goods and services and thereby make it easier for the debtor countries to acquire means of payment—but only to an extent that could be accommodated without seriously disturbing the domestic situation. The achievement of adjustment was by no means infallible or assured, at least between capitalist countries where private interest rules and private consent is required. Gradualness and mutual farsightedness, moderation and good will were essential when the required adjustment was difficult. When these were lacking—as in the attempt to collect immense reparations from Germany, or vast sums on debt account from our associates in the war of 1914-18 —the machinery broke. The economists, in presenting their idea of its operation, attributed to their fellowmen a greater degree of these qualities of judgment and fairness than they proved to possess. This is not the only connection in which they made the same mistake.

The economists tended to presume that international monetary and financial operations would work out satisfactorily though there existed a variety of monetary laws and standards as between the different countries. It was deemed that international economic activities would, except for secondary differences, shape themselves much the same way no matter what the monetary standard in individual countries.

This corresponded to the view that the international monetary system was primarily only a medium for facilitating commercial and investment activities. Emphasis was constantly placed on the fact that in its ultimate nature trade is, and always must be, an exchange of goods (or of services) for goods (or for services). Insistent are the warnings in the literature that the fact that a monetary medium was used should not obscure this basic fact. It seemed necessary to stress this continuously lest it be concealed by the fact that each trade transaction was an independent one executed in money terms. Still, compelling belief was not won. Many peoples and governments, as they wrote, continued to make extreme exertions to circumvent it.

However, during the period of development of this doctrine, the gold standard, of a type similar to that which existed in the United States up to 1933, was established in more and more of the trading countries. This shift toward uniformity and the further tendency to use the pound sterling as a common medium of account and payment throughout much of the world, made it natural to rest reasoning upon the assumption of a uniform standard. There was a buoyant expectation that this assumption would ever more closely approach reality.

Further, the international gold standard seemed an

excellent arrangement for the international movement of commerce. It seemed to effect most satisfactorily exchange between the many different national currencies, each valid only within one country. It appeared ordinarily to operate so as to favor stability in a relative exchange value of different currencies, which was on the whole favorable to trade, though freedom of the exchanges proved to be more important than fixity of rates. It seemed an efficient instrument for shaping within each country and between countries that specialization of economic activity that served the advantage of all. It was judged the appropriate monetary measure for economic relationships that had a truly international purpose.

For these reasons, studies of the course of trade under other circumstances—as under conditions of inconvertible paper money or under the silver standard—were left to specialized studies and monographs, as representing only secondary investigations of major tendencies.

HOW THE COURSE OF EVENTS SEEMED TO MATCH THE PATTERN

I have tried to summarize the doctrine that ruled the minds of the students of my time. This scheme of things laid bare, evoked admiring response and great hope. It must not be thought that this formulation was put forward by minds that were isolated from their contemporary world. Its main authors knew the laws, the policies, and the men of their times. They lived, in fact, in the midst of revolutions and of wars almost as disturbing as those of our days. The hope of effecting improvement gave impetus to their creation.

During the latter part of the nineteenth century and the pre-war years of the twentieth, events seemed to demonstrate the soundness of their analysis and to make their arguments effective. Invention and the improvement in methods of production and construction led to a great growth in production. New forms of power brought within human reach many new types of economic achievement. Cheaper forms of transport made possible much trade that cost had previously checked. Capital accumulated rapidly; flexible forms of business organization arose to undertake more extended tasks and risks.

The policy of governments continued in the main to favor the realization of the pattern for which reason had reached to permit it to operate with less interference than before. Tariffs and other types of trade restrictions were first reduced, and then, though later somewhat increased, remained moderate. The control to which the movements of gold in and out of countries were subjected was much reduced. Government intervention in the foreign exchanges disappeared—except for occasional central bank activity. The international gold standard spread its field of operation. The commercial agreements negotiated between governments gained in importance, and they tended to become an international system of accords. In a growing measure the rule of equality as between countries was adopted; agreements between countries for the exchange of exclusive trade advantages dwindled in importance.

The record of the growth of the world's commerce seemed proof of the great possibilities of the stream of trade interchange. That trade increased as follows:

WORLD VOLUME OF INTERNATIONAL TRADE,
1840–1929

Year	Total Imports and Exports in Billions of Dollars
1840	2.8
1860	7.2
1880	14.8
1900	20.1
1913	40.4
1929	66.7

Source: *Encyclopedia of the Social Sciences*, Vol. VIII, p. 194.

So international economic relations extended in accord with the thought that had been set forward. The results seemed roughly to correspond with those that had been promised. The shortcomings and mistakes were all too little recognized. It was left to other times to emphasize some of the ugly consequences of the course of change—the character of life in ugly and overcrowded cities, the new uncertainties, the wasteful use of resources, the great inequalities in wealth and income. In the older industrial countries, resentment and revolt, which had been active earlier in the nineteenth century and had then subsided, were brewing against these consequences. Problems had been created for which men later would press for a solution. But in 1914 it appeared to most that the pattern of international economic relationships which I have set forth was on its way to fulfillment. The world seemed reasonably content with its results.

Twenty-five years later it is in pieces. The pattern, both of fact and thought, seems completely submerged. There has come in its place, as MacIver said, "the wrathful separation of one from the rest."

II

THE DESTRUCTION OF THE PATTERN

THE COURSE OF DESTRUCTION, 1914-1940

I HAVE tried to summarize and interpret the analysis of international economic relations that formed the standard version of my time. Its revealing reasoning and great promise of universal benefit drew many fine minds into devoted elaboration of intricacies and refinements. Brilliant expositors propounded its essentials in universities, in trade and finance. Prime ministers, kings, and presidents were inspired by it in discussing with their peoples the possibilities of peaceful and stable international relations. For a time it seemed roughly to correspond to reality and to indicate the path of assured progress.

But now that whole structure of international economic relationship is in fragments. The nature and methods of international trade and finance, the relationship of governments to private activity, the bases of arrangements between governments, have all undergone great change. Today, in almost all countries outside of the American hemisphere, international trade is comprehensively regulated, if not actually conducted or dictated by governments. International movements of capital have ceased. The international gold standard no longer operates. The foreign exchanges are under most rigorous government control. The pattern of relationship has been torn apart as might be an umbrella in a storm. Those who carry it seem to hold but a bare intellectual staff with flying bits of cloth and uncovered ribs pointing to the sky.

I wish briefly to review the course of change—the road to the present. Then we may appraise again the doctrine, to understand wherein its explanations and judgments may have been faulty or inadequate, and to mark clearly what contrary purposes and forces have dominated those upon which the analysis counted for realization.

The great war of 1914-1918 did not seem either gravely to impair the validity of the reasoning regarding international economic relations that had previously established itself in men's minds, or to mark the end of the previous trend in those relations. True, in the documents that issued from the war there was scant recognition of any need of great determination and common will to re-establish the doctrine in fact. The only clause in the Covenant of the League of Nations that has to do with economic matters is merely a statement of principle imposing no immediate obligation upon any government. The states of Europe undertook to renew their economic relations after the war without any common binding economic policy.

The previously prevailing conceptions and methods struggled to emerge again as a pattern for the post-war period. Except in Soviet Russia, students repaired to the same body of thought and put it forward for the guidance of their countries. International commodity and money markets again began to function on a vigorous scale. The machinery of international commerce and of international payments resumed its operation. Gradually, legislation enacted for war purposes was repealed in country after country. The discriminations against the vanquished states came to an end. Many treaties and agreements lessening trade restrictions were negotiated between countries. Currencies were stabilized and became freely exchangeable for each other. Restrictions upon gold movements disappeared, and that metal again served as the primary medium for the settlement of international balances—although under much closer control of central banks than before. It seemed as if the vitality of the former scheme of relationship had proved itself, and that it would survive the terrible struggle and exhaustion of the war.

The resumption of international economic relations was much facilitated by the foreign lending and investment of the people of the United States. This country became, during the twenties, the main provider of capital for the whole world. We purchased the obligations of scores of governments, national and local. We became the possessors of promises to pay of foreign railways, public utilities, banks, and iron and steel plants. American investors supplied Germany, for example, with new reserves for its banking institutions, with working capital for its factories, with new plants for its exhausted industries. It undertook similar loans and investments in France, Belgium, Italy, the Scandinavian countries, and even in the newer states of Europe like Poland. It responded to the needs or desires of a score of Latin-American republics. American industry established branch plants in great numbers in Canada, and in lesser numbers almost everywhere else. The development of oil fields, mines, and even of plantations and ranches in various parts of the world was undertaken.

This flow of American capital was of great importance in increasing production in many countries and in enabling them to buy and sell more from each other and from us.

This contribution to post-war convalescence now appears to have been a useless one. From the point of view of the private lender or investor, it has not been the total loss that it is frequently represented to be. Interest and dividend payments received on our long-term foreign investment over the past ten years alone have been 5,760,000,000 dollars. Still it is plain that it was undertaken without sufficient understanding that foreign investment can only work out satisfactorily if international commercial and political relationships are in satisfactory shape. At the time it was believed that we were helping to assist toward order and appeasement. Now we perceive how strong were the forces of fury, resentment and fear beneath the post-war exhaustion. After twenty years we realize that few, if any, friendships, few outposts of national strength firm enough to stand the storms of today were gained. To have hoped otherwise was, perhaps, naïve. Lending and investment transactions, which in their original execution are hailed as of important national use, become in time half-forgotten business deals. The toasts are forgotten. The interest tag remains.

During the same period of the twenties, the League of Nations, through its subordinate economic and financial organizations, strove with diligence to make effective a program of international economic relations that seemed to correspond to its assignment for maintaining international peace. It conducted, with the help of economists of many countries, extensive studies of the causes and effects of restrictions upon international economic relations. Time and again the representatives of governments were brought together; and time and again the effort was made to secure simultaneous action of governments toward that end. Once, in the 1927 Convention for the Abolition of Import and Export Prohibitions and Restrictions, success was almost secured.

By the closing years of the decade, however, there were clear signs that many countries were about to impose new trade restrictions. The laments of the economists, the meetings of experts and government officials, failed to check the tendency. New tariff increases began to be recorded, now in the statute books of this country, now in the statute books of the next. Ideas, conditions, and purposes stronger than those that found expression in the pattern of international relationships began to have their way. In many countries piecemeal increases of tariffs were made. Then the United States, though its exports far exceeded its imports and the whole world was indebted to it, enacted the Smoot-Hawley tariff. Because of the effects of this action, other countries felt impelled similarly to raise their barriers. France began to apply the system of quantitative control of imports known as the quota system. The components of the British Empire, meeting at Ottawa in 1932, followed the same course and increased the preferential advantages each extended to the other to the disadvantage of foreign countries.

With the continuance of the depression and the gradual political doubt and bewilderment that spread over Europe after Germany and Italy put forward their challenge, many countries imposed new restrictions and controls over the transactions between their citizens and those of other countries. True, the United States began in 1934 its program of negotiating reciprocal reductions of trade restrictions. A few other countries like Sweden persisted stubbornly and successfully in their course of commercial and financial freedom. Great Britain and Japan increased their restrictions only moderately and as necessity seemed to compel; most of the Latin-American countries showed a similar reluctance. However, over most of the continent of Europe, and gradually over the world outside, the system of restriction and control was more intensely employed. The reductions in tariff which had marked the triumphs of the "free-trade" era were completely offset. The use of quota or licensing systems spread from country to country. By decrees and orders of various kinds, numerous governments began to prescribe directly the use of domestic products, both in consumption and in manufacture. For example, mills were required to use quantities of domestic cereals in making bread; refineries were required to dilute gasoline from alcohol and other substances for use as motor fuel; textile manufacturers were compelled to combine synthetic products with the natural textile fibers.

Each country—large or small, with a variegated trade or highly specialized one—was possessed of great uncertainty. The countries that live by producing mainly raw materials, such as wheat, cotton and wool, or copper, were unable to sell their products except at miserably low prices. Their capacity to purchase abroad enormously declined. The more industrialized countries found both domestic and foreign markets for factory products greatly shrunken, and idle workmen in crowded cities expressed their despair in claims upon their governments. The governments of various of the larger countries of Europe set about the attempt to stimulate the production within their boundaries, at multiplied cost, of the foodstuffs and raw materials they had previously imported—or substitutes for them. Between 1929 and 1933 the quantity of world trade fell by one-quarter and when measured in terms of pounds sterling, by well over one-half. This was enough to create suffering everywhere.

At the same time, international financial relationships were similarly smashed. Many governments took control of foreign exchange and permitted payment by their citizens to citizens of other countries only with official consent. Behind the installation of these exchange controls there was a variety of fears and purposes. In the countries that were greatly indebted to others, especially when the debt was collectable at short-term, the possible withdrawal of frightened capital threatened to bring about the complete destruction of currency value. Governments with the specter of the great German inflation before their minds did not dare face such a possibility. The financial failure of Austria in 1931 brought to an end the League of Nations' most promising experiment in financial reconstruction and brought near-panic in all financial affairs. Not long thereafter, the German Government established complete control of its foreign exchanges and began to devise that extraordinarily involved multiple currency system with which we have become familiar. Other countries imposed control over payment in the thought that it was a more satisfactory way of checking imports than other methods; still others resorted to it as a useful instrument for bargaining.

One result was that most international investment became jeopardized; new investment ceased; the payments for goods sold to many countries became hard to obtain. Almost universally the export of gold became subject to government permission. The link between currencies that the international gold standard had created was broken as regards a large part of the world. The process of effecting balance in the economic relations between each country and others, and the process of bringing about adjustment between their currencies were no longer an outcome produced by private calculations and activities. Governments took over the task.

Each step taken by each country affected the position of other countries. Each constraint of commerce or of payment imposed by any government tended to provoke or to compel similar action by others. The blows fell upon all. On shipboard, in times past, crews used to amuse themselves by arranging fights between half a dozen or more stripling sailor apprentices. A pillow case was tied over the head of each. They were put into a ring, with or without gloves. A gong was struck and each blindly tried to protect himself against the swings and lunges of the others. None knew, as he drew back his arm, whether he was going to swing at the air, or whether he would hit something solid, and if so, whom or what. But their situation compelled them all to swing and dodge until breath was gone and the gong was mercifully struck again. So countries acted in the conduct of their international economic relations during the depths of the depression.

The World Economic Conference which met in London in 1933 was a desperate effort to straighten out this tangle of affairs. It ended in confusion and each country was left to face its difficulties and nourish its resentments. The disintegration of the pattern of international relations continued, although economic conditions gradually began to improve in many parts of the world. For, unfortunately, the course of economic improvement coincided with an increasing strain in the political relations in the Far East and in Europe, with a growing menace of war.

Practices and philosophies that had previously been defended only on grounds of necessity and emergency were now in some countries made into the basis of proclaimed national policies. The objective of re-establishment of extensive relations with other countries was rejected as neither wise nor desirable. In the proclamation of these ideas, Italy and Germany assumed the lead. New merits were claimed for the idea of "national self-sufficiency," and the word "autarchy" found its way into every language.[1] Soviet Russia had for years restricted its commerce to what was deemed essential for the purposes of the state. Italy and Germany, and other countries in their train, endeavored to pursue substantially the same line. Whether and to what extent economic necessity dictated this course, or whether or to what extent it was but one phase of preparation for war may long remain a subject for dispute. The truth is probably that seeming necessity sug-

[1] The term "autarchy" had long been familiar in German technical literature, but had never attained general use. Gustav Schmoller in his important essay on *The Mercantile System* (1884), p. 62, explains that the phrase was suggested by Aristotle's description of the state as "having reached the end of entire self-completeness."

gested the first steps of the course, and then political purpose entered to intensify and glorify it until it became an end in itself for which every sacrifice could be asked. Certainly in these countries the ideal of an armed state, possessing all that might be necessary during time of war, was made paramount. The great and harsh might displayed on the fields of Belgium and Holland and France filled the hungry vision.

As the underlying character of international economic relations changed, the nature of the commercial agreements between governments changed—though up to the outbreak of the war the main agreements, not only of the United States but of the British Empire and the Scandinavian countries, were still of the pre-war type. The new types of agreements—whose characteristics and methods of operation I wish later to try to set forth in some detail—were different from the older types in various respects. They concerned themselves with new types of restrictions rather than only with tariffs; they often included provisions tantamount to direct government interchange; they often specified not only the conditions under which trade between the contracting countries could take place, but the methods of payment therefor. In effect, if not in intention, they were what are termed "bilateral" arrangements of an exclusive or semi-exclusive character. The trade opportunities that the contracting countries granted to each other in these agreements were not automatically extended to other countries; the contracting governments were left free to negotiate similar exclusive arrangements with other countries.

The hostility between nations that took definite form within the last few years, and the wars that have been fought and are being fought, intensified the rigor of all national controls. As plans for conquest were matured and fed with passion, hatred and fear mastered all else. The conflict in the Far East has made trade with that region primarily a wartime trade, governed by the purposes and conditions of war. The Italian conquest of Ethiopia, and the movement toward the use of economic sanctions which took place at the time, embittered commercial relations. As the German political program developed and the powers of Europe struggled with it, as the preparations for attack or defense became more and more frantic, as force asserted itself in Austria, in Czechoslovakia, and in Poland, the requirements of war became the all-decisive rule in the economic relations of all these countries within the possible circle of the on-coming war. Their trade and their finance were put in military uniform.

Outside of this American hemisphere, the whole present and the whole future have been and remain in issue, at war. Though we are not engaged in the immediate fight, its course and its outcome are of the greatest moment to us. The future of international economic relationships, and the direction of American policy, must depend upon what sort of world emerges from the war.

So events have run; so the present situation has come into existence. The great effort to realize the beautiful pattern of international relations was lost in a world of war. The doctrine of the past speaks on in textbooks like the voice of a religion whose practice has been put aside. The daytime, working-day imagination that fuses economic reasoning is at a stunned halt. The planes dart at each other in the skies. "Conquer or die" is the ruling order of the day.

It is useful and, to any student imbued with the doctrine of the great pattern, almost compulsory, to appraise the causes of its failure to prevail. Three different types of reasons may be discerned, even by the hasty measuring glance. First, it seems clear that the doctrine failed to take into sufficient account certain characteristics of economic life within nations that made certain of its conclusions dubious, and hence weakened its convincing force. Second, it always has faced and probably always will face the resistance of the interests and groups within each country which might suffer at any given time by the operation of international economic relations in the way the authors sought to direct them. Third, and most decisively, the nature of the international economic world is shaped by political and social events. These brought deep and bitter disturbance. In these three realms of national behavior lay, I think, the main explanation of why the fine pattern of international economic relations conceived by the economists was never but incompletely realized, and why action, even before the outbreak of this war, was so often directed differently from the course set out by the economists who attempted to advise.

As far as the explanation lies in the economic realm, primary emphasis may be placed upon the imperfect way in which economic systems have operated. The doctrine of international economic relations that has been set before you rested on the assumption that countries would achieve, and perhaps with short interim periods of disturbance, maintain conditions of full employment for all. This was in accord with the accepted reasoning regarding the operation of systems of free private enterprise. But in fact, there occurred in all countries frequent, and sometimes prolonged periods of depression, marked by much unemployment, unused productive capacity, actual or potential surpluses of goods, and heavy financial losses. Even in good times the fear of a coming of bad times has been present. For the past two decades, at least, there has been in most countries a chronic condition of uncertainty regarding the near and further future.

This uncertainty weakened the confidence of the rich and dominant. It disposed wage earners and farmers to resort to government action for aid, and in many regions of activity to supplant private activity by state ownership or control. Peoples and governments have been afraid to trust sufficiently to the outcome of that process of change and adjustment through which, according to the economists' account, the labor, resources and capital of each country would find their best and most rewarding use. Under these conditions, the rapid and assured shifting about of capital and labor as dictated by conditions of competition, and to make the most of new economic opportunity, did not come about. Resort was had, instead, to other measures. The fear persisted that imports, especially of competitive products, would mean a net and lasting loss of employment. A premium was placed upon any action or policy that seemed to promise increased immediate employment even though on poorer terms than those which might be secured in the longer run by the exchange of goods with other countries. Time and again experience might show that attempts to create employment by creating new restrictions on imports, forcing or stimulating other countries to do the same thing at the same time, were no solution for the problem of unemployment. But circumstances gave incentive to constant renewal of the attempt. The search for employment even on a poor level of productive result proved more urgent and dominant than the search for greatest possible national income. Nations were willing to employ two men to make at home a product that might have been obtained from abroad in exchange for another product that could be made at home by one man, because they did not know how else to employ the labor of the other man.

The same conditions intensified the almost universal wish constantly to expand exports. The employment provided by exports became in popular conception the only reason for international commerce, however often the economist might assert that the chief gain lies in the desirable goods procured through such commerce. This great exertion to export expressed itself in all manner of special means to promote exports, such as bounties, subsidies, and currency depreciation. Often this forced export trade threatened dislocation elsewhere because of its unexpectedness and the fact that it could not be met by ordinary business adjustments. Thus it often greatly stimulated an increase in the restrictions that it was designed to surmount.

In short, nations did not fully succeed in gearing together their production for domestic use, their import trade and their export trade, into a well-oiled self-adjusting piece of machinery such as the economists visualized. In their failure they resorted to the use of what they thought was a more direct, though perhaps less powerful, gear system.

The resistance to imports and the advocacy of self-contained national economic units were naturally voiced most stubbornly by those in every country whose interests seemed threatened by imports. Such groups strove to establish themselves in complete control of their domestic market. They clung to the hope or belief that profit could be made in the domestic market even though the whole national economic situation might be adversely affected by the confinement of commerce with the outside world. The groups combined their influence to make their interests prevail.

The assertion of group interests within each national state did not come solely from groups whose occupation and incomes might have been adversely affected by imports. In a less direct and less observed way, when the pressure either of growing population or unemployment was severe, the resistance tended to become general. Then, unless foreign demand for a country's export products is of a distinctly favorable kind—by which is meant of a growing trend and responsive to price reductions—the employment of greater numbers either in existing export trades or in easily established new ones is ordinarily possible only by lowering substantially the prices asked and rates of pay. It happens that export industries often prefer to maintain their price and wage levels rather than to seek greater volumes of sales at lower levels. This rigidity, as it is called, tends to create pressure for the restriction of imports as part of the effort to create employment. What happens in substance is that protective tariffs or other barriers are used to subsidize domestic production rather than to undergo such changes in prices and wages as would be necessary in order to employ more in producing for foreign markets. This is particularly likely to come about when export prospects are unfavorable.

With all these manifestations of particular group interests, the economist had long been familiar. He assumed as his task the attempt to demonstrate and emphasize the view that through international commerce the total national interest would be best served, and that if it were so served in the long run, all groups in the country would be better off. But the underlying conditions of uncertainty and unemployment imparted a force to self-interested groups that governments were not able to resist.

I pass to another element of the explanation. Those who formulated the doctrine of international economic relations that has been summarized, often pointed out the great variety of differences between countries. But they insufficiently appreciated the importance of these differences, and the extent to which they lead to differences of policy as between countries. They underestimated the possible advantage to *some* countries at *some* times of forming *special* and perhaps *exclusive* economic connections. The uniform policy set forward as guide often could not provide the result that particular countries, with their individual difficulties and characteristics, at the moment wanted most. They turned to other possibilities, though often the advantage was temporary or illusory.

There are large states and small states, strong states and dependent states, well governed and badly governed states, contented states and discontented states,

states ready for war and states fearing war. Each of these differences tended to reflect itself in national policy, and had a variety of consequences. Sometimes policy has been partly determined by the necessities of preserving political stability within a country rather than by calculations of economic benefit. In other instances, the requirements of foreign political policies have ruled rather than economic calculations. In still others, this inequality between states has led to the conclusion, correct or incorrect, that even economic interests were best served by preferential or special economic relationships rather than by participation on equal terms in general world commerce.

The most satisfactory trading universe, according to the economists' analysis, is made up of great international markets in which the producers of all countries offer their goods on nominally equal terms, i.e., subject only to the same restrictions, and purchasers enter to make the best bargain. In such a trading universe the productive resources of each state would be gradually adjusted, if no restrictions were imposed, so that the products which each makes most advantageously find their way into the market while each draws from the market those things that it could not produce or produces only at greater cost. Under these conditions all states would tend to achieve the highest possible national income. This is the conception of and the justification offered for the rule of equality in international trade.

But to some countries at some times this may be or seem to be a hard road to travel. It requires adaptability and initiative; and the outcome for any one country depends somewhat on the readiness of various others to cooperate. Therefore countries, especially those which have the smallest variety of resources or are the less skilled and equipped with capital, or have the smallest reserves of gold or foreign exchange, seek special arrangements with other countries—whereby they may dispose of their products more or less irrespective of price. Thereby it is hoped to avoid adjustments necessary to meet the competition of others on a plane of equality. Such tendencies become all the more strong in times of shock and uncertainty. For then security and stability, rather than the attainment of a permanently high standard of living, become the ruling purposes.

The most complete network of special accords before the war was in Central and Eastern Europe, and the history of their making is a record of most intricate interplay of economic and political hopes and fears. The fact that some of these countries were primarily dependent on the sale of high-cost agricultural products made special offers of assured markets tempting. Thoughts of political consequences sometimes created a wish to abstain, at other times a fear to refuse—when the bargain was to be struck with a more powerful state. The smaller countries in making their decisions watched every flicker of strength and fortune among the larger ones. They sought and took economic advantage where they dared, avoided, if they could, engagements that might impair their safety, accepted others if refusal was too great a risk. The intricate and various measures that the statesmen trod elude the standard graphs and charts. They are left for epigram and anecdote.

The larger states of Europe went in for similar arrangements partly for the same reasons and partly for others. German and Italian policy was originally stimulated by the sense of necessity, of needing to have an absolutely certain market for exports with which to pay for imports. Later both diplomatic and military calculations gave imperative purpose to the same line of action; it was judged more important to develop economic relations with some parts of the world rather than with others.

Preferential arrangements contracted between the various parts of the British Commonwealth and Empire, to take another example, were similarly prompted partly by economic and partly by political calculations. The United Kingdom, at the cost of impairing its trade relations with many other foreign countries, and of increasing the trade difficulties faced by them, felt itself impelled to trade to secure more firmly its place in the markets of the British Dominions and Empire.

The United States had followed France and various other countries in increasing tariff protection; this British action was taken partly as offset. But in addition, it was probably thought that the preferential arrangements would make a large investment of British capital throughout the Empire more secure. And also there was the thought that as the separate elements of the British Commonwealth were acquiring an increasing degree of constitutional and political independence, special economic ties were well advised.

One more example: the trading methods of Soviet Russia have been in their very nature based on special arrangements. They have ordinarily been short-time trade agreements approaching closely the use of direct barter method. The products to be exchanged, and their quantities, have been directly specified. Considerations of price and of competition may be subordinated under this trading method. The possibilities of equal treatment become dim. Each agreement of this kind is a special agreement, and if equality of trading opportunity between the countries engaged in them is achieved, it would be by accident. The making and execution of trade arrangements become closely akin to the making and execution of political arrangements, and each state makes shift as best it can in the ever-changing game.

I have tried to illustrate the variety of circumstances and considerations which have prompted the resort to what I have called special agreements. It is plain in review that the economists' doctrine underestimated the variety of circumstances in which they might have conclusive appeal. It is plain also that if the universal trading system, based on the rule of equality, is again to become the prevalent one and bring about its possible economic benefits, there will be required some modification of the conditions which find their expression in special accords. The practice of the rule of equality is a mark of the fact that the world is established on an orderly basis, that small states can live independently, that large states renounce aggression, and that a general disposition to keep trade restrictions moderate exists. This is the type of world, no doubt, that was assumed by those who put forward their analysis of the pattern.

And thirdly, the economists' anticipation as to the nature of the international world has been completely disappointed. For a long time, the economists' judgment had been crowded by tumult and war, then by their fear that population would always grow so quickly that mankind would be forever in need. But these fears had gradually faded, and during the period when the great pattern was being most hopefully expounded, replaced by anticipation of a slow, steady improvement through the action of private enterprise in a peaceful world. Instead, war and social revolution again came to rule in much of the world.

These are some of the conditions and forces not adequately reckoned with in the standard doctrine of international economic relations. They have all played their part in shaping the events of the past two decades. My account of them is incomplete. It is also explanatory rather than appraising. I cannot assume the great task of reckoning whether and to what extent the policies and actions of any *individual* country were forced by these conditions along an inevitable course, and as to whether under the conditions this course was for it even sound national policy. Perhaps it is even beyond all effort to establish. But certainly the *general* result, the *joint* outcome of the policies and actions, has been a blunder and a failure.

For Germany and Italy alone, should they win the present war decisively, could there seem triumphant vindication of past policy. Only the oppressed, the dead and wounded could make eloquent contradiction.

THE TRAGIC SEQUENCE

In this field of history cause and effect create a tragic sequence. As commerce between nations is interrupted and declines, the standard of living and the chances of livelihood similarly worsen. Lack of opportunity, half-filled stomachs, lost savings, unemployment—all the cruel components of misery—make men more responsive to the idea of resorting to arms or revolt, even though it be against others equally or even more miserable. Those who advocate seizure by force from others, have despair to play upon. And despair is turned easily to hate of those who are to be attacked. There can be little doubt that economic deterioration and restrictions played some part in the involved movement of passions and interests that took the peoples of both the Far East and Europe into war.

And the ironic dilemma is this: That when once any country of consequence turns, or even strongly leans, toward such action, international economic relations are thereby further disturbed and economic suffering increased. Every other country, strong or weak, that feels itself threatened begins to face the possible necessity of having to defend itself. Each country devotes an increasing part of its working effort to military preparations, and trade becomes increasingly a trade in military supplies that does not improve the conditions of living. Governments subordinate such matters as sufficient food, decent housing and adequate clothing to procuring those things useful in war. It is guns, not butter, that are most wanted—a boast recalled on the battlefield. The items of trade are scrutinized and regulated, not in the scale of economic benefit, but in the scale of utility in the exercise of diplomacy or war. Increasingly the building up and equipping of air, land and sea forces, to conquer or resist, absorb the products of trade. Within a circle of states so engaged, international economic activity cannot bring about improvement of the conditions of life; it is highly controlled, hesitant, and a branch of military planning. The hour comes when there are enough food and warm clothing only in the trenches. The dead need no supplies.

Further, the geographic lines of trade are displaced. Governments seek to direct their trade where it serves purposes of diplomacy or combat, sacrificing trade that may be more economically advantageous but promises no political or military advantage. Again each item of the trade movement is scrutinized to determine whether it may help the potential enemy.

When the tragic sequence takes its course, the light in the economist's study burns low. The pattern of international economic relationships that he has evolved, half from observing what they were in peaceful times and half by dreaming of what they might be, becomes *all* dreaming.

I have tried to set forth the main reasons why that beautiful pattern of relationships that was woven by genius and carried forward so diligently by statesmen of many nations, is now so torn apart. We can see that no unseen hand, in Adam Smith's imaginative phrase, is at work inevitably to bring about its realization.

It is clear that if people ever wish to attain its ends and benefits, many acts and policies will have to be shaped to make it possible. First, in each country there will have to be tolerated in some measure the effects of competition even when readjustment of established interests is required. Second, countries will have to restrain acts and policies which vitally injure other countries and tend to compel them to take measures that broaden the field of injury. Third, the prospect of peace must be firmly established in the world; not a peace imposed by force, and kept by fear, but one wrought and sustained by just men.

III

INTERNATIONAL ECONOMIC RELATIONS IN THE ON-RUSH OF WAR

INTERNATIONAL TRADE BECOMES A TRADE IN LIFE AND DESTINY

I HAVE sketched the emergence of the prevailing discord in international economic relations. To appraise its significance a more thorough examination is essential.

One major change in the nature of international commerce is before all men's eyes. Most of its present movement is being dictated by conditions of war. This has vastly modified its composition and greatly affected its geographic movement. The Soviet Union and the countries at war and those who fear that they may be at war have placed their trade relations under complete government control. None has unlimited resources with which to buy foreign goods, and the resources of some are extremely limited. These governments, therefore, are restricting to an essential minimum imports of products for ordinary civilian use or for use in the production of goods for civilian purposes. They are devoting all else to the acquisition of goods that contribute to fighting strength. The consequence has been that the volume of trade with these areas in such products as tobacco and fruits, pleasure automobiles, moving pictures, radios and refrigerators, is much curtailed.

On the other hand, a large trade has arisen in arms, ammunitions and implements of war—especially in airplanes and airplane parts. Further, the trade in such metals as copper, iron ore, aluminum, tin and the alloys used in steelmaking has been stimulated. A vital premium rests upon the acquisition of petroleum supplies, although the total quantity of petroleum products that has moved in world trade may not have actually increased because of the restrictions upon the use of petroleum products for ordinary purposes.

The movement of this trade in war materials is determined in a wholly different way from the trade movement which has ordinarily occupied the economist's attention. Its demand is governed not by economic considerations but by military and political ones. Its potential size is limited only by the purchasing power of the countries that are seeking to build up their military strength, and by the course of the war. It is destined for a rapid increase, then must be characterized by a swift decline.

Economic considerations play little part in determining its geographic movement. That is governed by the strategic position of the belligerents and the operation of blockade controls and the conduct of actual warfare. The commerce carried on by Germany and the countries it has occupied is almost entirely with its land neighbors, while that of Great Britain and Japan is almost entirely an overseas trade, and that of free China is conducted only by circuitous overland routes in Asia. In the effort to make available foreign exchange go as far as possible, the belligerent countries to the utmost extent try to draw their supplies from their own national or imperial territories irrespective of price and cost.

Hard and forthright means are being used to acquire supplies. Small countries are being compelled to deliver by terror. The negotiators for the small Baltic and Balkan states have been afraid that refusal will bring an army over the frontier. Seizure after invasion has become an important means of supplementing deficient supplies. The ships that entered Bergen and Copenhagen discharged armies as cargo; the planes dropped gunners into Rotterdam. The merchants scattered before them. Their commerce was displaced by one in national destiny. It became soldiers' work, not traders.

THE CHANGED CHARACTERISTICS OF THE PRESENT

I have attempted to sketch and explain the emergence of the newer (by reference to our own times, for there are many close prototypes in former times) types of international trade method and relationship, and trace their establishment and extension as prelude to and part of war. Let me summarize more thoroughly the changes thereby brought about in international trade relations.

The large international markets that previously existed especially for agricultural products and the raw materials of peace have been either greatly reduced or have disappeared. In these markets the supplies of the world were formerly offered for sale on a competitive basis to competing purchasers throughout the world. It may be said that in an imperfect and incomplete way, the total world supply and demand situations for particular commodities found expression in these markets, and that the prices established therein were world prices—in a sense of being the same throughout the world, taking into account transport and other similar costs. The transactions that producers and traders conducted in these markets were guided by calculations of private gain. Thereby was determined how much of particular commodities were bought and sold, by whom, and at what price. The interaction between prices and the supply and demand situation determined the course and volume of trade. Such were the underlying characteristics of the trade movement when large and relatively unhampered international markets existed.

But now these large international markets have virtually ceased to exist except as regards some branches of trade that center in or about the American hemisphere. Trade relations now are marked by a different combination of characteristics.

First, the terms of commercial agreements made by governments have become far more influential in determining the trade movement than before. For when government action creates impassable barriers for trade, it is only government action that can lower the barriers so as to permit trade. The question of what trade is permitted and with whom and on what terms becomes decisively determined by agreement.

Second, trade in many countries is now to a considerable extent conducted by or for government account. Not only do intergovernmental agreements restrict and regulate more closely transactions that individuals may arrange; governments themselves have come to deal with many matters that formerly were left to private enterprise.

Third, competition between buyers and sellers of

different countries has become in many quarters less usual and effective than before. Under the conditions imposed by governments and war, buyers often can turn but to relatively few production sources, and sellers in particular countries can look only to similarly restricted markets.

Fourth, competitive prices have lost decisiveness in the areas of trade where such agreements and conditions rule. The prices at which the exchange of goods takes place in these areas are determined within a restricted field and sometimes by the dictum of governments.

Fifth, the exchange of goods has been made increasingly subject to the requirements of bilateral balance between pairs of countries. Formerly little thought was given to the relative size of the import and export movement between any two countries. It was usual that one country buy from another, without regard or concern, much more than the other country bought from it, while its trading position in regard to a third country was the reverse. For example, during many decades Great Britain bought a vastly greater amount of Argentine products than Argentina bought of British products; on the other hand, other purchasers of Argentine products, such as the United States, bought less than they sold to the Argentine; the sterling which the Argentine secured by the excess of sales in Great Britain could be freely used to meet obligations in the United States and elsewhere. Such trade is generally called "triangular" or "multilateral."

It has been largely displaced in the trade relations of many countries. These direct their policies, so far as they can, so as to bring about an equal balance of current obligations between themselves and each other individual country. Or as expressed in German explanations of the foundations of the present German trade policy: "The arrangement of reciprocal commitments between two countries as regards quantities of goods to be exchanged on the basis of just price relations." Commercial exchange that takes place under such agreements is in large measure different from that which had established itself previously as most favorable from a standpoint of private buyer and seller. It would have a counterpart in the domestic economy if, for example, New York required that residents of Mississippi buy the same amount from New York as the residents of New York bought from Mississippi, and both enforced severe control to assure this result.

When international economic relations become completely subject to the conditions I have outlined, producers and merchants can sell their products only where governments make it possible; the amount of their production and the return they may receive for it is largely settled by governmental decision, and the form and time of payment is dependent upon the arrangements their governments may make. Similarly controlled and restricted is the right to purchase foreign goods and to pay for them. According as to whether or not negotiators agree, a family may or may not be able to buy soap, procure tubes for its radio, have coffee upon the table.

When a system of private and relatively free commercial and financial relations prevailed, each country, as has been set forth, was exposed to the necessity of adjustment of both its internal economic affairs and its external trade relations. Where this kind of international system is superseded, the particular adjustments through which it operated may be avoided or at least postponed; but others of a different character almost certainly are found necessary. By means of special arrangements it may be possible for some countries to a substantial extent to isolate themselves against the interplay of international competition. It may be possible for them to sustain certain trade that would be lost under conditions of open private competition, usually sacrificing other international commerce to do so.

Among the consequences may be a loss of adaptability and of independence—save perhaps for the few most powerful states. The dependence of some countries on others has been accentuated. When restrictions were much less conclusive, and when there existed a world-wide flow of international commerce and finance, the producers of each country could look to extensive possible markets and conversely, each country had the world toward which to turn to buy the goods it needed. Comparatively wide distribution of trade meant comparative freedom and independence both in economic and political affairs for all. The smaller and the weaker countries shared this freedom and independence almost in the same measure as the larger and stronger ones— except in so far as their exports were concentrated in few fields. They could permit their commerce to flow according to the calculations of private enterprise and in the channels that on the whole represented the largest economic benefit. They did not have to fear that any other country, by refusing to buy or sell, could seriously injure their economy or dictate their affairs— except by protective tariff increases.

Now—with trade as much segmented and obstructed,

and governed by special accords as it is, producing countries often find but a limited market in which to dispose of the goods which represent necessary employment and income. They feel compelled to make whatever terms may enable them to acquire entry into such limited and restricted markets as are open to them, and to accept any necessary dependent connection. This is a matter of particular consequence to those countries whose exports are composed of a relatively few products. It is these considerations that created, particularly in the small countries of Eastern and Central Europe, and in those of Latin America, the sense of having to accept trade arrangements imposed upon them by important customers. The loss of independence may be only in the economic field. But in some instances it has assumed political significance.

THE NEW TYPES OF COMMERCIAL AGREEMENTS

The rapid extension of the newer types of trade agreements, and the prospect that the United States will have to adjust its policies and methods to take them into account, give importance to an understanding of their main features and details.

The formerly prevailing type of commercial treaty or agreement had two main elements. It set forth the maximum tariff rates the two contracting countries would apply to the exports of the other. It bestowed reciprocally the right to enjoy most-favored-nation treatment in commercial matters.

The types of accord now most commonly negotiated are much more full and complicated documents, dealing specifically with many other matters, and resting on a different base.

Any attempt to classify them must be somewhat arbitrary and inexact. There are endless blends and variations, and numerous different viewpoints according to which they might be classified. For purposes of summary exposition, however, I will place them in four groups:

1. The group whose difference from the older type is a matter of scope rather than of fundamental nature. This type might be called merely *the extended commercial agreement*. In contrast with the agreements of the past decade, agreements of this type attempt precisely to take into account, and set the terms of, not only tariff restrictions but the whole range of restrictive methods and devices that have come into use. They represent an exchange of obligations between the contracting governments concerning the maximum restrictions of the various types which each government may impose upon exports coming from the other. On the whole, they contemplate that the trade will be carried on between the private interests of the two countries, and that the discharge of payments will be carried out through the private financial system. In these respects, they differ at least in degree from the other types of newer agreements.

2. As the system of control and restriction of trade and of payments extended, countries frequently found that the types of assurances which they had carefully negotiated in agreements of this first type failed in fact to provide the full protection for their exporters or investors which had been envisaged. The safeguards did not appear sufficient *vis-à-vis* countries that, through exchange controls, prohibited or rigorously restricted the transfer of payments for goods imported.

Therefore it tended to come about that the countries in a position to do so sought firmer guarantees in some form of pledge which would assure their nationals of prompt payment. In many instances the original purpose was merely to assure payment, when due, for export trade that already existed; this was often supplemented subsequently by another—to acquire new export trade. To effect these purposes, countries in an advantageous position sometimes threatened in turn to restrain payments for imports from others and in some instances actually resorted to such action to secure a satisfactory negotiated agreement.

The loosest of these are known as *"payment agreements."* They may be separate agreements or merely part of more comprehensive trade accords. Their essential feature is that they determine, in part or in whole, what use may be made of the foreign exchange proceeds that accrue to one country as a result of its exports to some other country.

There may be cited as instances of this type of agreement numerous arrangements which the United Kingdom has negotiated with other countries. For example, in the agreements negotiated between the United Kingdom and Argentina since 1933, there are specifications as to the uses to which the sterling proceeds acquired by the sale of Argentine goods in the British market are to be put. It is specified that after a reasonable deduction required by the Argentine Government to meet the service of its foreign debt outside of the United Kingdom, the rest of the sterling should be set aside to pay for Argentine purchases of British goods, or for the shipping services of British vessels, or for the payment of interest and dividends on Argentine securities in British possession. Another example is the agreement that existed between Great Britain and Germany before the war, whereunder Germany agreed to proportion the total sterling acquired from the sale of German goods in Great Britain to pay for current and past commercial obligations to the United Kingdom and also to maintain service on the Dawes and Young loan obligations, retaining only the remainder at its free disposal.

To the extent that such arrangements prevail, it is plain that the foreign exchange acquisitions of a country are in reality "blocked exchange," not free exchange; they can be used only in the agreed-upon fashion and not freely according to the desire of the possessor. This means some loss of choice either to private individuals or to governments.

This type of agreement to some extent must influence trade toward bilateral balance; for it assures payment for imports from some countries while leaving payments for imports from other countries uncertain, or even unlikely. A partial or complete bilateral balance of accounts between the countries entering into a payment agreement is enforced.

The operation of payment agreements requires the keeping of records and the frequent interchange of information between the contracting governments as regards the fulfillment of the terms of the agreement. However, the actual discharge of the payments arising out of import and export trade can be and usually is left to the private international money and financial markets. Each individual transaction is carried out by the parties directly concerned. This is in contrast to the more rigorous and complete form of agreement regarding the making of payments that are known as "clearing agreements."

3. The characteristic *"clearing agreement"* provides that payment shall not be made directly by or to the individuals concerned in the trade transaction. Private international financial arrangements are superseded. Intergovernmental arrangements are established for direct periodical clearing of the *total* sums due to the nationals or residents of each from the people of the other. The matter is usually handled this way: Each government requires that its citizens having debts to meet in the other country pay the sums owed, in the currency of their own country, into special accounts in an institution designated by the government. Deposits into this account ultimately discharge the indebtedness so far as the private individual is concerned. Each government then pays out of the account, again in its currency, sums due its own people by the people of the other country. The agreements usually contemplate that the two governmental accounts will be periodically cleared as against each other; surpluses, due in one direction or other, being permitted or disposed of in the manner set forth in the agreement. As a matter of fact, it has often occurred that as one side of the account runs up heavily against the other the exporters of the country to which sums are owing restrict their sales, lest payment to them be indefinitely delayed.

Let me illustrate by an example of a rather inclusive character—the agreement signed between Switzerland and Germany in 1937. This provided that the residents of Germany, having payments to make to Switzerland for goods and services, should pay in German currency the amount owed into an account carried in the

Reichsbank, the official German central bank. Correspondingly, residents of Switzerland having payments to make to Germany were to make these payments in Swiss francs into a special account in the Swiss National Bank. The clearing was then carried out as follows: The sums paid into the Swiss National Bank—which made up a fund of Swiss currency—were reserved to pay out again to residents of Switzerland to whom payments were due from Germany in the following order: Of the total amount accruing in the Swiss account 3.5 million francs monthly were to be paid out of the account to cover the expenses of German tourists in Switzerland; the balance of the receipts remaining thereafter was to be allocated as follows: 17 per cent to make payments upon various German external debt obligations owned in Switzerland, 53 per cent to pay for exports of Swiss origin, 10 per cent to cover incidental export costs and the remaining 20 per cent on other debt accounts. To complete the picture of the arrangement it should be added that German exporters to Switzerland receive payment from the Reichsbank out of the German funds paid into the special account by German importers of Swiss goods. Even this bare recital of only the most essential details will bring home the elaborate degree to which in some of these clearing agreements governments determined the disposal of foreign exchange that came under their control.

When the trade relations between the two countries are regulated by either "payment" or "clearing" agreements, experience has shown that there is a tendency for the exchange of goods (or services) between them to be forced toward equal balance, even though no such tendency existed before. Sometimes this comes about because the country that has the stronger bargaining position uses it to increase its exports to the other country. But more generally thus far the equalizing has occurred on the downside—except when a military purpose gave special impetus and one or both countries were insistent upon securing imports for this reason. Where and when both contracting governments may be intent upon developing the exchange of goods between them, and are ready to make the required adjustments the balanced trade may be forced to a higher level.

There is no inherent reason, it may be observed, why "clearing" arrangements between separate pairs of countries might not be woven together into joint accords. Tentative efforts to establish such an arrangement are in fact being made by the German government. It is seeking to "clear" its accounts with countries such as Switzerland to whom a recurrent surplus of payments are due from Germany, by proffering payment in the form of balances obtained by Germany in its clearing accounts with other countries now under German occupation such as Holland. It is probable that in these first efforts Germany is testing the possibility of operating, under its direction, such a system for the whole of Europe should the German conquest be complete. Any such arrangement might be a counter-part of political and military domination. Such domination would convey the power to dictate trade currents and the forced re-making, no matter what the cost and suffering, of the economic life of each included country. The interests of any or all particular groups or areas would be subject to the dictating will.

Where economic life remains under the direction of private interests, and governments remain free, the difficulties of operating any such multilateral clearing system would be much greater but not necessarily impossible. A difficult and constant negotiating effort would be required to arrive at the terms and methods of adjusting payments between countries—which was once done effectively through the international monetary system.

A sense of great common need, or of determination for joint defense, might draw free and independent countries so closely together that they could make the system operate. But if that sense or determination exists, the growth and maintenance of fuller economic interchange between them—for which monetary arrangements are but the instrument—could be attained without establishment of a system of intergovernmental clearings. Where the will exists to increase trade, and to pool financial resources and economic effort, numerous direct measures to effect that result lie at hand. Where this does not exist any system of governmental clearings can yield no result commensurate with the restraints it imposes. Such a system is, in itself, but one of various possible ways of handling "old debts." Under certain circumstances it might supplement rather than supersede private international financial arrangements.

4. In the case of the fourth of the newer types of

agreement to which I would call attention, the creation or maintenance of a strict equality of in-payments and out-payments is the express basis of the agreement; hence its name *"compensation agreement."* The characteristic of the compensation agreement is the definite provision for the exchange of designated and offsetting values or quantities of specified products for each other.

The contemplated interchange may be carried out under the direction of or through the agencies of the governments themselves. Or it may be left for private traders in the two countries to engage in the designated exchange. A simple example of the earlier type of compensation accord is that negotiated between Hungary and Czechoslovakia in 1932 in accordance with which 29,000 Hungarian pigs were admitted entry into Czechoslovakia in return for the admission by Hungary of 20,000 carloads of wood fuel, and 1½ million crowns worth of eggs laid by Hungarian hens were admitted to breakfast tables in Czechoslovakia on the condition that Hungarian tourists would spend in Czechoslovakia the amounts necessary to pay for the eggs.

A somewhat more refined example is found in the agreement negotiated in 1939 between the Italian and Argentine Governments; therein it is specified that if the imports of either country from the other exceeded by more than a small margin the reverse movement of goods, that country should then be free to restrict imports from the other with a view to restoring equality. The Italian Government notified the Argentine Government under this agreement of the amounts of various

Argentine products which it would admit into Italy during 1939, and the Argentine Government, correspondingly, adjusted the imports it would admit from Italy.

In the sense that all of these types of agreements, in greater or lesser measure, condition the purchases of one of the contracting countries directly upon the purchases of the other, they all partake of the character of barter agreements. There are, besides, recently negotiated accords, which are both in form and substance outright *barter accords*. The Russian-German agreement, negotiated just before the war, for example, is apparently of that character. Its details are not fully known. But it apparently consists of a direct arrangement for the exchange of designated physical guaranties of designated goods—so much petroleum, so much foodstuffs, etc., for so many units of specified manufactured products. The direct exchange of oil for rayon between the Mexican and Italian Governments may be cited as a further example.

It has become by no means unusual that important parts of trade agreements should be kept secret or semi-secret. What is published may by no means fully indicate what is unpublished. What is written may be less important than what is unwritten. If the terms agreed upon are communicated to the business groups affected, that is done only under strict seal of secrecy. This is a mark of the tenseness that has come to characterize the negotiation of commercial accords. Information that only a few decades before it was deemed essential to reveal so that private enterprise might turn it to the fullest advantage, it has now sometimes become treason even to whisper.

This account is sufficient to show how and to what extent, in some parts of the world, various governments have abstained from no type of restriction upon their economic relations that might be useful in enabling them to wrest advantage from others. Negotiators walk into conference halls fully armed with the whole of the state's power.

THE FORCES DIRECTING THE HANDS OF THE SIGNERS

References have already been made to the variety of forces and purposes that have led countries into these types of agreements. To review them adequately would require a separate analysis of the recent history of each and every country. In the case of Soviet Russia, the governing fact has been that agreements of this mode were most compatible with the complete control of economic life by the state. In the case of Germany, different forces or calculations have been dominant at different times. During the earlier thirties National Socialist theory was reinforced by the difficulties that were encountered by Germany in conducting trade with neighboring states in which many control measures had been established, and partly as a result of the pressure of other countries to collect on investments in Germany. In the later thirties German commercial policy was framed as a counterpart of political and military design to acquire control over Central and Eastern Europe and to assure supplies in event of war. Overextended debt and unstable monetary situations were primary conditions in shaping the course of some small European states like Hungary; and with still others it was their desperate search for a market for certain raw material products which they produced at much higher costs than overseas producers, and whose price had fallen during the depression more than the price of the goods they imported. In the case of Switzerland, the policy appears to have been adopted primarily because it was judged the best method for retaining markets for Swiss goods, which were of a specialized character, and also as an instrument for collecting on foreign investments. Various Latin American countries have taken some steps along the same path, largely as a result of the great difficulties encountered in finding markets for their raw material products even at depressed prices, leading to the necessity of accepting payment in blocked currencies. This is an insufficient and oversimplified account of the economic stresses and strains, the combinations of economic and political purposes, that led to the making of the new varieties of accords.

Many countries, learning from current experience that, as all of them resorted to special agreements, all but the powerful were exposed to an unsatisfactory, unsettled economic existence, might well have found the way for concerting their policies along more satisfactory lines if it had not been for the re-entry of war in the world. But Japan engaged in its great struggle in the Asiatic mainland, Italy undertook the conquest of Ethiopia, the Civil War began in Spain, and brought out sharply the danger of a great division, and Germany marched into Austria and Czechoslovakia. Each of these events ruptured trade and financial relations, and each hurried on the preparation for war. Economic relations became increasingly subordinate to military ones and frequently just a part of them. The most important pre-war European trade agreements, such as that between Great Britain and Turkey and that between Germany and Russia, were decisively shaped by military considerations. They foreshadowed the battle of the tanks along the Meuse.

The commercial agreements that have been negotiated in recent years accurately reflect the state of the world—more than half at war and affording neither security nor stability in economic or political affairs. They make up an infinitely criss-cross and clashing accumulation of obligations, bearing clearly the marks of the urgency, the fears, the rivalries, and the threats which have gone into their making.

When trade restrictions were comparatively simple, and trade agreements were roughly uniform in character, resting on a most-favored-nation basis, the agreements negotiated by different countries formed an interconnected whole. Tariff reduction agreements did not cover a whole tariff, but between them they normally covered most of the typical products of the countries which indulged in the tariff bargaining game. The exchange of most-favored-nation privileges was a safeguard to all against the exclusive bargains that might be struck between others. Controversy was not infrequent, and tariff wars were not unknown; but the controversy usually marked the failure of countries to agree. Now it is often the negotiation of an agreement that creates the conflict situation. For when restrictions become as manifold as they are at present, and com-

mercial agreements become exclusive in character, even
under favorable conditions harmonious adjustment between the agreements of different countries would be
difficult to attain. Under existing conditions almost
every country is engaged in a free-for-all struggle in
trade matters against the rest. In this time of war,
the struggle has assumed, in many parts of the world,
the deadly seriousness of war. The visit of a foreign
trade delegation today, in many countries, is a mo-
mentous event not only in its economic but also in its
political destiny.

THE PLACE OF GOLD AT THE PRESENT MOMENT

In the Middle Ages, gold—the precious metal and
prized means of payment for other goods—was stored
in chests. When harvests failed, or armadas had to be
financed for foreign expedition, the chests were emp-
tied. When enemies pressed against the castle walls,
chests were hurriedly transported to what was deemed
a safe place.[1] As a consequence of the tumult of recent
times, the distribution and handling of gold have become essentially the same as in those far past times.

During the years a private international system of
commerce and finance operated without too drastic
restriction, gold was widely distributed among the different countries of the world and was mainly in private
possession. Quite substantial amounts were to be found
in at least a score of countries serving as the basis of
monetary and credit structure. I give for example the
distribution of the world's gold in 1913.

---

[1] The world has never witnessed a flight of gold as great as that in
recent months from France and England to the United States and
Canada. A substantial part crossed the Atlantic on battleships.

DISTRIBUTION OF MONETARY GOLD
END OF 1913

(In Millions of Dollars)

	In Central Banks and Treasuries	In Circulation and Other Banks	Total
France	679	1,021	1,700
Germany	296	699	995
United Kingdom	170	600	770
United States	1,290	634	1,924
South American countries	344	76	420
Japan	67	19	86
World	4,811	3,818	8,629

Source: *Encyclopedia of the Social Sciences*, Vol. VI, p. 692, Article "Gold." (Based on data in the *Interim report of the gold delegation* of the League of Nations, 1930, pp. 114 ff.) The table ignores most of the gold in private hoards, especially in Asia and Africa. The world total shown in the table excludes India and Egypt entirely.

The flow of its movement between countries was gradual and comparatively small. Except under emergency conditions, governments gave little heed to it. A man might carry a purse of gold pieces across ten frontiers and never have to explain to a customs official.

All this is now changed. During the past ten years so enormous a movement of gold from the rest of the world has taken place that over two-thirds of it is lodged here in this one country, and much of the remainder seems to be on the way. This was sent to the United States partly in payment of the billions of dollars worth of goods and services that we exported in excess of what we have imported. The rising demand for American goods needed for defense and war increased the excess. Secondly, social discontent, high taxation, depreciating currencies, and war led the people and governments of other countries to send their funds here for safekeeping. Third, there has been a growing foreign investment in American securities. These have brought to the United States over 20 billion dollars of gold and carried the gold supplies of all but a few countries down to a scant minimum.

This movement has been expressive of the anxieties that have beset the rest of the world and of the strains upon their resources. It has been accomplished by a constant extension of government restriction of gold movements. In fact, gold everywhere has been requisitioned by governments. The individual store that all through history has been held as last protection against adverse fortune, private or public, is no more. It all rests in a few great government vaults. The owning governments decide where and whether to employ it for the making of international payments.

Except as regards transactions centering around the United States it may be said that the international gold standard has ceased to function, and even here it has no longer some of its main attributes. In some countries gold is no longer even the nominal base of the national currency system; in others, where it has been retained as nominal base, monetary and credit policy are directed independently of the gold position. In other words, although still in universal use for making international payments, gold is not now an important activating or regulating element in the monetary and credit situation of individual countries. Its movements between countries do not at present bring in their train adjustments in the trade relations between individual countries as they tended to under the international gold standard. Under the operative international gold standard, gold served first as a valuable commodity with which payments were discharged and, secondly, its movement was an important activating element in tending to bring about equilibrium in the relationships between each country and others. Now it serves only the first function—that of prime medium of payment in the international exchange of goods and services.

Formerly it might be said, as a general proposition, that the purchasing power of units of gold, in terms of units of other commodities, was determined by the supply of gold and the demand for it in its several uses. This was always a very qualified and loose relationship. Now the purchasing power of gold, at least within individual countries, is established primarily by government decision, and is nominal rather than actual. It varies substantially from country to country because neither it nor other goods can move freely. American purchases have sustained its value everywhere.

It may be noted in this connection that in a similar fashion exchange rates between the currencies of at least some countries have become largely a matter of government declaration. Restrictions on the movement of gold and goods prevent adjustments in trade relations that might make the exchange rate an actual expression of them; and on the other hand, exchange rates are prevented from changing by government control. This affects in many ways the commerce of all countries concerned, but it is impossible within our limited opportunity to go into this complicated technical subject.

It might be further observed that for various currencies, even for some important currencies such as the mark and the pound, there has come into existence a variety of exchange rates. The student of the trade agreements to which Germany is a party for example will find that the mark is valued differently in various agreements. Such differences can be maintained either because the mark figures in these trade arrangements merely as a convenient accounting device while actual payments are made through governmental clearings; or because of the close controls maintained upon the exchange of currencies. Furthermore, the mark has a different value in different uses; for example, marks that may be used to purchase goods in Germany have a far higher value in terms of foreign currencies than the mark that may be used only for travel in Germany. Thus in an international sense a mark is not merely one currency but many different currencies. More recently even the British pound sterling has two values; the pound sterling that may be employed in transactions over which the British exchange control has taken charge has one value in terms of the dollar; the pound sterling which can be acquired on the free market and used for other purposes has another value.

Under these circumstances there are obviously no reliable international monetary relationships except as they may center around the dollar. Each national currency floats in its own national medium, and those international ties which used gradually but firmly to settle their *relative* levels have grown much feebler. The fixity of the dollar in terms of gold is the only stable base of reference that now exists.

INTERNATIONAL CAPITAL MOVEMENTS UNDER PRESENT CONDITIONS

The movement of private capital for investment across national frontiers has practically ceased. Virtually all recent international loans and investment undertakings have been carried through by governments.

The collapse of private international capital movements is a natural result of the ruling uncertainty. The grave risks of war that have prevailed in many places, the deterioration of public finances, have reinforced the doubts created by the restrictions upon commerce and the foreign exchanges. There have been few parts of the world in which these cumulative risks and obstacles have not seemed too great to overcome the hope of profit.

These aspects of the matter are obvious and need no elaboration. Attention may be called to one of the less easily perceived of the new difficulties. It has been pointed out that when there was an international system of commerce and finance, operating under conditions of comparative freedom, the balance of payments between individual pairs of countries was of secondary consequence. As long as an investor in a foreign country felt secure that that foreign country's power to acquire foreign exchange anywhere in the world was sufficient to enable it to meet its obligations, he did not have to reckon further with the matter of transfer. This is different now. Owing to the growing tendency of countries to put their relationships with each other on a bilaterally-balanced basis, and to the strict control over the foreign exchanges, it has come about that the investor in many parts of the world can look confidently toward receiving his interest and dividends only if his own country, by imports or otherwise, provides sufficient exchange for the borrowing country.

To put the matter in more technical terms, transfer relationships, as well as other economic relationships, have, as regards various countries of the world, tended to become bilateral. The remittance of debt service or the yield on investments has become in many instances a matter determined by intergovernmental agreement. For example, each of the European countries whose citizens had large investments in Germany made separate terms with Germany in behalf of its nationals only, as one of the conditions of continued purchase of German goods. American investors in German securities were left out of these arrangements, though in many cases the securities they held were part of the identical issues held in Europe. An instance of another character is the policy pursued by the Spanish Government in regard to permitting the transfer of dividends and repayments of short-term credits; it has made it possible for such transfers to be effected only when and as special commercial inducements were granted, or when the creditor country was in a position to exact payment.

Exaggeration must be avoided. The extent to which many debtor countries sustained up to the outbreak of the war the practice of equality as between the investors of different countries has been, considering all the difficulties, rather remarkable. Thus it will be found that Europe west of the Rhine, the Scandinavian countries, Italy and Poland, and Austria and Hungary in the main, and Japan, and the British Dominions, and almost every country of Latin America have made conscientious efforts to accord equality as between bondholders of different nationality in regard to payments on long-term loans and investments. There have been greater and more numerous discriminations in regard to the discharge of short-term investments.

Private international lending and investment of recent years have been extremely small. In fact the reduction by debtors of the volume of their external loans and the repurchases by debtor countries of foreign investments within their borders have exceeded the new loans and investments.

Recent international financial operations have virtually all been carried out by governments. They were undertaken by governments who were willing to assume risks that private capital would not assume; sometimes they were extended with the thought of increasing exports and thereby giving employment to their own people, or of responding to the urgent economic need of some friendly people, or to achieve a political purpose. Most of the international lending transactions carried out by European governments have been intimately connected with political arrangements or agreements.

The lending activities of the American Government have been carried out through the Export-Import Bank. In the main, its loans have followed the same forms as private transactions of a similar character. American exporters have sold on credit, and the Export-Import Bank has furnished the necessary funds or underwritten the risk. When credit was thereby extended to countries exercising control over their foreign exchanges, the Bank has usually asked and obtained concrete assurance that the government of the borrowing country would permit the transfer of interest and principal. In other transactions, loans have been directly extended to foreign governments.

Some of the loans made by other governments have been closely linked with trade arrangements. Not infrequently designation has been made of the goods to be bought with the proceeds of the loan—which does not differ in substance from the practice followed by the Export-Import Bank. But some of the agreements specify as well the goods which the borrowing country shall send to the lending country at some future time in discharge of the debt. Such a financial arrangement might be called a "barter loan." The loans extended by both England and Germany to Turkey may be cited as examples.

In some current economic literature, especially German literature, the latter type of arrangement is hailed as a much superior method of international finance, on the ground that it eliminates all possible repayment difficulties, and also wipes out "interest slavery." In underlying essence, it merely means that the lending country, at the same time that it arranges the loan, assures the borrowing country a definite future market for products the value of which might be sufficient to pay the debt. Such arrangements, if they work, eliminate any transfer difficulty as regards the particular transaction; they safeguard the borrowing government against the possibility that repayment may be made more difficult by increases in trade restrictions. The idea, therefore, is basically sensible. It should be understood that the same result is achieved, while binding both parties less rigidly, when lending countries pursue commercial policies that accord with their creditor position. Unless a country is prepared to pursue a commercial policy consistent with its desire to have its foreign investment prove sound, foreign investments should be foregone or loss anticipated.

The question of "interest slavery" is an empty one. If a government wishes to make a foreign loan without interest, that can be done under any form of loan agreement.

This, then, comprises, as far as I can achieve it, a review of the main characteristics of present international economic relations. It has been an analysis of division and disorder in the midst of which individual countries pursue their economic and political aims with great intensity, seeking, against all rivals and enemies, trade or victory.

The United States stood somewhat apart from these developments and the disorder, but its present condition and its future situation is gravely affected by them. Its position has been, or seemed to be, somewhat unique. Why that is so, in what respects it is so, to what extent our policies can be shaped independently, are the next matters I wish to consider.

THE UNIQUE POSITION THAT WE SEEM TO HOLD

THE HAZE IN WHICH WE LIVED

AMID the turbulent reshaping of economic relationships between nations that took place during the twenties and thirties, the situation of the United States was in many respects unique—or at least so it seemed to most Americans. The conditions under which this country might direct its international economic policies seemed more favorable than those in any other country. We were less touched by the pinch of war, less conscious of the hand of fear, less disturbed by political discontent. Thus there seemed no need to depart from our customary ways. Our situation appeared to entitle us to think—even if we did not always act—in terms of economic welfare. We could entertain the belief that our difficulties would solve themselves; we could attempt to keep flying banners that fell from other hands.

True, the situation was favorable only by comparison. The actual circumstances which prevailed during the twenty years between wars were in no sense free of trouble. The United States experienced depression or semi-depression during a substantial part of the period. The world with which it had to deal was in upheaval, and toward the end of the period moved by revolutionary doctrine and intense struggle. These disorders in the outside world themselves, it is now plain, made the achievement of satisfactory permanent international economic relationships impossible.

Turn for a moment to consider the general attitude toward international affairs that ruled in the United States during the period. This country was free of any aggressive political purpose; hence its trade and enterprise were welcomed everywhere. Apprehensions that had previously existed in various Latin American countries that our economic expansion might be a prelude to political domination were largely allayed.

We were at peace and desirous of so remaining. The country in general had no fear that its security or form of government might be threatened from the outside. The perils that beset others, Americans commonly regarded as through an opera glass—a drama that we watched from our seats. The choice of living at peace, out of range even of the most carefully devised attack, seemed to all save a few, definitely ours. Hence the country judged it unnecessary to participate in any collective effort to organize and enforce international peace and order. Such participation was rejected on the score that it was not necessary to protect our own position and might require us to take part in wars arising out of quarrels between other countries. We watched, some with distress, some with equanimity, the gradual falling apart of the European structure that had emerged after the last war. We stood aside from events elsewhere, letting them shape their outcome without any vigorous intervention on our part.

At the same time we neglected to take the measures needed to place this hemisphere beyond danger against the possibility that outside events should shape themselves to our disadvantage. An easygoing isolation seemed enough to most Americans; and we were content in a half-hopeful, half-anxious haze.

Amid this haze it was not to be expected that we should arrive at clear-sighted and coherent determination of international financial and economic policies. Some of our major actions in this field—such as our rigid stand in the matter of intergovernmental debt settlements and the increased tariff protectionism of the twenties—reflected the opinion that we need not concern ourselves with what happened in the outside world. In fact some of the advocates of these policies regarded the resultant injury in our relations with other countries a good in itself. Other policies, such as our program of foreign lending, and the persistent effort to sustain our foreign commerce, were, on the contrary, influenced by the hope that they might contribute to world stability and peace. A vague notion existed that our dollars could perform the tasks that might otherwise require human lives.

The same general sense of security made it appear unnecessary to impose restraints upon our dealings with other countries lest their actions strengthen them and weaken us. So, too, it seemed unnecessary to organize our economic and financial interchange for use as an instrument of national power amidst the struggle in which others were engaged. We were guided by our general disposition to avoid enmities and to build friendship on trade. Only as the present war has revealed how incomplete our security is, and how dominating may be the force that ruthless men have made out of new industrial techniques, have we begun to take new reckonings.

Throughout virtually the whole of the period there prevailed an insistent and diversified demand on the part of the rest of the world for American products. Our producers were ready and able to supply a greater range and variety of products to foreign purchasers, on good price terms, than those of any other country. We had emerged from the war of 1914-1918 with a greatly expanded production of farm products. In a variety of minerals, as in the petroleum field, skill in extraction and refining and the large amounts of available capital for effective world-wide sales organization, enabled us to acquire a primary place as suppliers. And most definitely, in a hundred branches of manufacturing, such as automobiles, American products excelled, and often were the cheapest.

Persistently the world ordered more American goods than it could pay for. Thus, we have never had to feel anxiety about possessing the means to buy those foreign products which we desired. This made it unnecessary to strive with the same vital intensity as other governments to secure by special agreement or otherwise, particular sales opportunities or markets. True, surplus problems at home led us into various extra aids to export; but even these were marked by restraint and the hope that improved world conditions would make them temporary. Therefore we were enabled to stand somewhat apart from that urgent clamor and conflict of special arrangements in which most of the rest of the world has engaged. Similarly, this underlying condition left us free of any necessity of maintaining control over our foreign exchanges or of the movement of funds between this country and other countries. I am not forgetful of that short period in 1933-1934 when, as a merely temporary emergency, such action was deemed essential. This was in my judgment a brief crisis connected much more closely with our domestic business and financial conditions than with our relations to the outside world.

The immediate difficulties that filled this period were rather those to which a wealthy nation is exposed. The fact that so many branches of our production could, without seeming to enter into the realm of unsound business calculation, look to the outside world for markets, created a persistent tendency to endeavor to export more than others could pay for. This protracted situation accounts in part for the ease with which the United States followed a course of extravagant and careless foreign lending during the 1920's, which in turn sustained the export movement.

The gap between foreign desire for American goods and foreign purchasing power inevitably meant the exercise of a choice among our products. The choice expressed itself through the ordinary operation of commodity and financial markets. Foreign production and participation in world trade increased relative to American in branches where our comparative advantage was least, as, for example, cotton, copper, wheat, shoes. But in addition, foreign governments cut off various imports from the United States by increasing their restrictions upon them; and in many instances they directly undertook to supplant American products with others, either by subsidizing home production or by giving preference to imports from other sources.

The consequence was, of course, not only to keep our total export trade within bounds, but also to curtail some branches of it more than others. The demand for farm products proved stationary relative to the greater elasticity of demand for manufactures, for metals and for oils. Long before 1914 the relative importance of agricultural products in our total export trade was on the decline. That trend was checked during the period of war demand. But in this post-war period it again clearly manifested itself. Other areas, in Canada, Australia, Argentina and Brazil, with newer soils, became competing sources of supply of many of our agricultural products. Other countries found it easier to dispense with American agricultural products than with various American industrial products.

AGRICULTURAL EXPORTS[a]

(excluding forest products)

Yearly Average or Year Ended June 30	Per cent of All Exports of United States Products
1877–81	80.1
1887–91	74.6
1897–1901	65.8
1907–11	53.8
1917–21	42.6
1927–31	35.9
1937	26.2
1938	26.5
1939	24.0

[a] Statistical Abstract of the United States, 1938, p. 623.

This stimulated the support in some agricultural circles for export controls, for resort to subsidy methods, and for proposals whereunder the United States might dump its agricultural surpluses abroad irrespective of price. It also partly explains the agricultural policies of the American Government. These, in general, were a courageous and foresighted attempt to deal with the consequences of stationary or declining export markets for agricultural products. They definitely lessened the latent clash of interests between the United States and other countries. Furthermore, the favorable disposition shown by the American Government toward efforts to establish international agreements for the regulation of the production and export of such commodities as wheat and cotton was prompted by the same circumstances and desire. So, too, one of the chief objectives of the Trade Agreements program was the wish to restore foreign markets for our agricultural products.

OUR NATIONAL INTERESTS AND PURPOSES

The national interests and purposes, which during this period between wars received most attention in shaping our economic and financial relationships with the rest of the world, were few and simple. They all continued to stem from the tree of belief in the suitability and feasibility of restoring that pattern of relationship that had prevailed before 1914.

We desired for use and need for production many products that we did not produce, or that we did not produce to the full extent of our need except at a decidedly higher cost than that at which they could be purchased abroad. But during this period the United States encountered virtually no difficulty in obtaining such products or in having adequate funds to pay for them.

We had need to conduct with the rest of the world a substantial, and if possible, expanding volume of export trade. Many branches of American production, production on the farms, other raw material production, and industrial production, as organized, required foreign markets for part of their output. The alternative for each and every one of them was unsatisfactory. It was a prospect, at least during a period of some duration, of equipment unused, of men and women out of work, of prices depressed, and of surpluses bringing ruin to their producers while mocking at want. This was not really a matter of scattered local importance, as it is sometimes tempting to assert or believe. The total of American production of movable goods which were sold in foreign markets was but a small fraction of our total production—in the neighborhood of 8 per cent. But the number of our main occupations included in that fraction is large. It included such main sections of our agriculture as those producing cotton, tobacco, rice, corn and hogs. It included our oil producing regions. It included such enormous industries as automobile, radio, machine-tool, and refrigerators. It affected the volume of traffic on our railways and the activity in all our port cities and in our merchant marine.

Substantial declines in the foreign business of these branches of production would have affected—at least during a period of transition—the whole competitive situation in each of these branches of production, the whole price situation, the whole employment and wage situation. These in turn have an effect upon all aspects of other businesses of both the farm and the city. It should be unnecessary to trace out the intricate and sensitive lines of influence by which the course of our foreign commerce, as it has been organized, affects the whole of the national economic condition. The story-book method of doing so is the most simple and the most familiar. The farmer who before going to bed listens to weather reports on the radio—with his growing corn or fattening cattle in mind—might study also the reports of the movements of ships in the port of New York. The latter, in just as direct a way as the weather, will enter into the determination of how much he will receive for his months of work. So too the skilled carpenter, wondering whether there will be houses for him to build in his small town along the seacoast, might well be interested in the question whether our cotton is still being used in foreign mills.

When our export commerce declines, in the absence of some countervailing change, the burden of relief and readjustment, at least for a period of some duration, tends to fall upon the national government as well as upon local ones and to shape national policies as well as local ones. Let me again resort to an elementary illustration. Ever since the opening of the broad Mississippi plains, a substantial part of American wheat was produced to sell abroad. In recent times other countries have increased their wheat production, some fitted by nature to do so and others by means of great special subsidies. It results that the place of American wheat in the world's markets has become much restricted. The existence of a high tariff—42 cents per bushel—does not solve the problem for the surplus-producing industry. The national government must grapple with the problem. It is led into plans for the regulation of production, for the making of payments to compensate for reduced production, for the use of Treasury funds to subsidize exports. Even then it watched that stream of lonely and displaced figures that John Steinbeck has made us think of as Okies make their way across the dusty plains to the Pacific Coast; and it must concern itself with their miserable plight and suffering.

In summary, taking the distribution of our productive effort as it was during the twenties and thirties, the maintenance of a substantial volume of foreign commerce contributed toward domestic prosperity and lessened the burdens of change thrown upon the people and the burdens of relocation, rebuilding and relief thrown upon the government.

During the period under review a national interest of another order came into existence. As a result of the war of 1914-1918 this government became a creditor of various European governments in very large amounts. We chose to try to collect the principal of these war loans with interest. The originally loaned principal was approximately 10 billions of dollars. The total of annuities arranged under the debt settlements to run through sixty-two years was 22 billions. During the twenties private American citizens loaned and invested further billions of dollars abroad. This process of foreign lending and investment continued for about ten years in an irregular but enormous jet. Repayments on old investment took place while new investment was being made. Securities changed hands between the nationals of different countries with great frequency. Attempts to value certain of the investments, such as those in oil fields and branch plants, can be made in a variety of ways. Therefore, exact computation of the total of our creditor position at any given moment is uncertain. But at its greatest height, in 1930, before repayments and repatriations had really attained substantial volume, before defaults on loan obligations had begun to occur in large amounts, before properties were lost through war or repatriation, the sum total of privately held obligations exceeded 15 billions of dollars.

This combination of holdings of the obligations of other countries and of ownership rights to properties in other countries made the United States—say in 1930— the greatest creditor country the world had ever known. This fact was at the time taken in the main with pride, complacence and a sense of prosperity and economic benefit. All these loans and investments, it was hoped, would yield to the government and people of the United States a steady and substantial stream of return by way of payment of interest, of dividends and of repayment of principal. Without any further work or exertion on our part, as a nation, we would be in possession of the means of acquiring from abroad large amounts of desired goods and services.

As far as thought was given to the matter at all, there seems to have been a general presumption that the task of transfer involved in the making of payments on these loans and investments would take care of itself as smaller amounts had in the past. The world and its commerce were undergoing a steady expansion. The international trading and financial mechanism during the twenties seemed to have regained much of its former vitality. It was anticipated, except by skeptics and critics, that debtor countries and creditor countries alike would permit such adjustments in their economic life as were necessary to make possible payments and the acceptance of payments. This would have meant, according to the former scheme of adjustment, relative shifts in prices and wages in countries with debts to meet so that their exports would grow and yield the foreign funds required to pay debts to us. As a counterpart, it implied relative increases in wages and incomes in the United States, and a relative growth in our purchases of foreign goods as compared with our exports. Commercial and financial policies here and elsewhere, it was optimistically conceived, would be suitably adjusted. This was a mistaken judgment, and our foreign investment has suffered. But it still remained of importance and claimed consideration if that fortune were not to be dissipated.

I have cited specific and commensurable national interests. There are others of a less tangible character— which had great influence in shaping our attitude and policies. I will not attempt another foray into the question of the part played by economic conditions in the shaping of history in deciding whether nations remain at peace or go to war. There are many voices in the throat of nations, many longings and passions in the spirit, many dreams in the mind. No one knows which may rule. But it seems clear that, at least in some instances, satisfactory economic conditions are conducive to strengthening peaceful policies and purposes on the part of peoples and governments, and miserable and disturbed conditions increase the likelihood that they will resort to measures, the consequence of which may be war. It seems clear also that satisfactory economic conditions usually make for stability in the form and operation of governments and favor the maintenance and practice of individual liberties and political institutions resting on individual liberties. On the contrary, great economic need usually tends to sharpen internal struggles, produce political instability, and create a readiness to suppress individual liberties.

In this connection, a wise and foresighted nation must weigh many facets and make a careful appraisal of many possibilities. It will not make the mistake of believing that an aggressive and hostile country will find sufficient satisfaction in the return from trade to modify its purposes or feeling. It will not sacrifice its security for some measure of extra trade. But within such limits of caution as the state of the world may demand, it should be ready to share, through trade, the yield of its resources and productivity with others. It should be ready to offer a world whose peaceful intent can be trusted whatever it can in the way of economic opportunity. And violent social revolution anywhere in the world is disadvantageous to us. We must contribute, if the chance exists, to an orderly social program.

And lastly, the feeling was entertained that even for a country as powerful as the United States, the good will and a sense of mutual interest on the part of other countries were an important national consideration. If we are heedless of the needs of friendly foreign countries, if our policies unnecessarily shut them off from our resources, we prejudice our relations with them. A country that does not concern itself with the plight or problems of others, does not grasp opportunity to serve useful benefit, casts away influence. Others will step in to seize it, if they can. How firmly, of course, any influence based upon friendly ties will stand unless supported by force equal to any that might challenge it is one of the grim and bitter speculations toward

— 91 —

which this year's events propel the mind. Who dares to have weak friends in a world of quick rising terror?

These are general maxims and reflections regarding the national interests and purposes which were active in the period between two wars. Ahead of the nation was that swift and tremendous change in circumstance which few fully foresaw, and which many sought to deny or refused to recognize. In a day when circumstance can change so quickly, a nation must develop the capability of appraising anew its interests and purposes equally quickly. We have cherished peace, prosperity, and advancing social welfare—comfortable in the thought that our independence, security, and internal stability were safe beyond threat. We know now this is not so.

SOME FEATURES OF AMERICAN EXPERIENCE 1920-1940

American trade expanded markedly during the twenties. Exports exceeded imports by substantial amounts. The onset of the depression expressed itself in the swift decline of both.

Even in the early twenties American commercial policy was not well adapted to the permanent maintenance of a large export trade and a creditor position. What followed was an intensification of that policy, originating as an attempt to deal with the difficulties confronting many branches of agriculture that did not share in the apparent prosperity of the industrial regions during that period. This led to tariff increases in 1921 and 1922. Though these had failed to improve the agricultural situation, another demand arose for still higher tariffs on farm products. It found its outcome in a widespread and substantial upward revision

Yearly Average or Year	EXPORTS[a]			IMPORTS[a]		
		VALUE			VALUE	
	Quantity Index[b]	Index[b]	(Million Dollars)	Quantity Index[b]	Index[b]	(Million Dollars)
1921–1925........	97	96	4,397	94	89	3,450
1926–1930........	122	105	4,777	116	104	4,033
1931–1935........	76	45	2,025	92	45	1,713
1929........	132	115	5,241	131	113	4,399
1930........	109	85	3,843	111	79	3,061
1931........	89	53	2,424	98	54	2,091
1932........	69	35	1,611	79	34	1,323
1933........	69	37	1,675	86	37	1,450
1934........	74	47	2,133	86	43	1,655
1935........	78	50	2,283	106	53	2,047
1936........	82	54	2,456	118	63	2,423
1937........	105	74	3,349	131	79	3,084
1938........	105	68	3,094	94	51	1,960
1939........	110	70	3,177	108	59	2,318

[a] The index numbers given in this table are based on exports of United States merchandise and on general imports through 1933, imports for consumption thereafter. The dollar values given, however, are for exports, including re-exports, and general imports throughout. These dollar figures are the ones most frequently used in general descriptions of our foreign trade.
[b] 1923–25 average = 100.

of the tariff in the Smoot-Hawley Act of 1930—extending not only to agricultural items, but also to a wide range of imports in any way competitive with the products of American exports. Further, in separate legislation excise taxes, that were really tariffs, were imposed on copper, oil, lumber, coal and vegetable oils. Foreign debtors found it harder to meet their debts, easier to plead inability to do so. Our economic relations with the rest of the world were struck with new uncertainty and new misunderstandings.

The country continued to struggle with the problems of improving and restoring its international economic relations. Up to the outbreak of war there were many reasons for the belief that they were slowly being rebuilt and that the difficulties in this field were gradually being overcome. This was in part just an expression of our own great economic vitality and flexibility. It was in part the outcome of the new direction given to our commercial policy. Heavy losses were suffered. Many painful adjustments were made; many others remained to be made. The expenditure of public funds had been great and prospective future burdens remained heavy. But some useful lessons had been learned; some important new methods devised for dealing with economic emergencies; some new foundations had been built for our social structure, as for example, the social insurance system. Recovery in our international economic relations seemed to be in the making; and the steps that might be required in the future did not appear to be either so urgent or extensive as to mean fundamental change in our lives.

The chief act of modification in our international economic policy was the passage of the Trade Agreements Act in 1934, since renewed in 1937 and 1940. This Act authorized the Executive to negotiate agreements with other countries for a reciprocal lessening of trade restrictions. It empowered the President to reduce existing tariff rates (down to 50 per cent of the existing rate) and to obligate the government not to increase rates or impose new ones—in return for corresponding improved treatment of American exports. Under this authorization the American Government between 1934 and 1939 entered into twenty-two agreements with foreign governments, of which nineteen are still in effect. These agreements were negotiated, in each instance, after a careful study on the one hand of the position of the American branches of production whose tariff rates were under consideration, and on the other hand of the prospects of securing increased trade for various American branches of production. Each negotiation was preceded by detailed reports by expert officials within the government, prolonged discussion of these reports by committees made up of interested government departments, and presentations by the representatives of the American producing interests that might be affected by tariff changes.

The trade movement comprehended within the field of the agreements by 1939 had attained considerable importance. It is reckoned that these agreements dealt with the terms by which 30.3 per cent of our export trade with the world (on the basis of 1937 trade data) was determined and 59.7 per cent of our import trade with the world. Under the terms of the agreements the American tariff rate was lessened by varying percentages from very minor changes to the full authorized 50 per cent on 18.9 per cent of our imports. The government gave guarantees covering 2.1 per cent of our total imports that duties would not be increased and that the duty-free status would not be changed on items constituting 38.7 per cent of our total imports. In a few instances, the tariff modifications were safeguarded by quota arrangements which limited the quantity of the foreign product admitted at the reduced tariff rate, notably the quotas on cattle and petroleum. The operation of the Trade Agreements Act brought about no fundamental change in our own method of regulating the movement of foreign goods into this country.

In return for these modifications of our own trade restrictions the government secured lessening of restrictions on the part of other countries and safeguards against future increases of restrictions. However, the problem of defining and satisfactorily formulating these conditions to be accorded American products by other countries proved far more complex than that relating to our own action. In many of the agreements the government had to take into account not merely the tariff structures of other countries but their intricate maze of quota systems and of subdivided quota systems used for bargaining purposes, of exchange controls and of subdivided exchange controls used for bargaining purposes, administrative regulations, the operation by other governments of purchasing monopolies of various sorts, and lastly the effect of the special bilateral agreements to which most other governments have become parties. The contrast may be illustrated this way. The governments of other countries have had to try to negotiate themselves *over* our high and rigid tariff wall; the

United States has had to try to negotiate itself *through* a dense jungle of obstacles that shifted every night.

In negotiating these agreements the United States has been ready to extend to each and every country equality of treatment in the American market. In other words, it adhered to a system of single tariff rates to be applied to the goods of all countries, except those which may discriminate against us and from whom we may, if we choose, withdraw the privilege of equal opportunity. This, more technically, is known as the unconditional most-favored-nation policy. As a counterpart, the endeavor was made in each agreement to assure equality of opportunity for American goods in the foreign market. Of all the problems of negotiations, the attempt effectively to attain this was the most perplexing. It would have confronted us, of course, no matter what our commercial policy, no matter on what lines the Trade Agreements Act had been administered. It is important to American producers because, given equality, their productive abilities assure considerable success. It is advantageous because it lessens the conflicts, favoritisms and potential antagonisms of a rule whereby different countries are treated differently, and affords a basis for an international system.

Our foreign commerce during the period of the operation of the Trade Agreements Act increased. No man can measure how much of the increase was the result of the lessening of restrictions brought about by the operation of this legislation and how much of it is a result of other circumstances. But there can be no doubt that as a consequence of having moderately lessened our own trade restrictions, foreign purchases of American products were definitely greater than they would otherwise have been. The lessening of trade restrictions by other countries made possible export business that otherwise would not have been possible; it created a willingness to turn purchases in our direction rather than away from us; and it provided some of the funds to pay for purchases in this country. In all of these ways it acted, up to the outbreak of the war, as a factor in the rectification of our international economic relationships.

The war, of course, has brought to a halt the negotiation of new agreements. American trade with some of the countries that had most readily entered accords with us, the Netherlands, Belgium, Sweden, Czechoslovakia, has ceased. The three major agreements with Great Britain, Canada and France remain nominally operative, but the course of war governs the trade.

The formulation of our future permanent commercial policy is, for the hour, in suspense. It has become subordinate to our general policy toward the course of war and to our defense effort. It has become dependent upon the outcome of the war and the political and economic situation that will follow.

ADJUSTMENTS IN FINANCE AND INVESTMENT

I turn to other phases of adjustment in American economic relationships since the depth of the depression.

Modifications in the relative value of the American dollar and various foreign currencies was one of the elastic factors in the situation. The preponderant weight of payment between the United States and the rest of the world was toward the United States. The

demand for American goods, accentuated by the advent
of war, and the mass of foreign obligations held by us
and the flight of capital to the United States, expressed
itself in a constant need for dollars, while the falling-
off of markets, especially for certain of the raw material
producing countries, the disorganization of production
or its devotion to military effort in many other countries, constantly tended to impose a limitation on the
amount of dollars available. These facts and many
others have tended to make the dollar a "strong" currency. The value of the dollar in terms of gold was
reduced by approximately 41 per cent in 1933-34. Ever
since, year by year, month by month, there has been
a gradual lessening in the relative value of most other
currencies in terms of the dollar.

FOREIGN EXCHANGE RATES
(Averages of noon buying rates in New York)

Month or Year	Pound Sterling	Franc	Lira	MILREIS Official	MILREIS Free Market
Jan. 1933	$3.3614	$0.0390	$0.0512	$0.0764	—
July 1933	4.6499	.0546	.0737	.0787	—
Jan. 1934	5.0493	.0621	.0831	.0856	—
July 1934	5.0407	.0659	.0858	.0844	—
1935	4.9018	.0660	.0825	.0829	—
1936	4.9709	.0611	.0729	.0857	$0.0588
1937	4.9440	.0405	.0526	.0872	.0618
1938	4.8894	.0288	.0526	.0584	—
1939	4.4354	.0251	.0520	.0600	.0512
June 1940	3.6016[a]	.0201	.0504	.0605	.0503

[a] Free rate; official rate 4.0350.

This shift was an accurate expression of the underlying commercial and political situation. It tended to
remove the stimulus given in 1933-34 to our export
trade and somewhat facilitated export trade of other

countries. Thus it prevented our excess of exports from being even more preponderant than it was.

Another underlying economic change of importance has been the debt adjustments that have taken place. In 1934 all of those governments that had borrowed from us during and after the war of 1914-1918, save only Finland, declared the task of payment too difficult under depression conditions and defaulted on their debts. This item ceased to figure among the elements making up our balance of payments. Many of the foreign investments made by private citizens of · the United States also fell into arrears or default. Germany ceased cash payment on all of the immense amount of the German securities held in this country except the Dawes and Young loans. Since its occupation of Austria, Czechoslovakia and Poland, the dollar obligations of these countries have similarly been unpaid. All of the bonds issued in this country by Latin American countries except those of Argentina, Uruguay, Santo Domingo and Haiti fell into partial or complete default for a shorter or longer period. A few of the so-called "direct" foreign investments were completely lost. Others under the conditions of the depression ceased to earn dividends. Still others had to delay the transfer of accumulated earnings or dividends until transferable dollars should become available.

These losses have been substantial and many private individuals in the United States have felt their gravity. There has taken place much repurchase by foreigners of securities originally sold by Americans, while these were in default or their prospects were otherwise dim, at prices much lower than those at which they were originally sold. This practice was even followed by some countries and governments at the very time that the plea was being made that interest or dividend obligations could not be honored because of lack of exchange. This and the more ordinary process of resale have reduced the principal value of our long-term foreign investment substantially—from perhaps around a peak of 15 billions to a current estimate of about 10 billions of dollars.

But it is a mistake to regard that course of private foreign investment as nothing but a record of loss. In fact, despite the obstacles we imposed on payment, a substantial part of it has become remunerative and some of it has yielded a handsome return. I cite, for example, the investments in branch plants in Canada and in the United Kingdom, the investments in the government securities of France, Belgium, the Argentine, Sweden, Norway and Italy. This list is by no means inclusive. The returns from these holdings of foreign securities and investments at their peak in 1929 were estimated to be about 979 millions. By 1932 they were 461 millions; in 1939 they approximated 525 millions. A constant flux takes place in the fate of particular securities. Substantial headway has been made in the last two years in adjusting the defaults of various Latin American countries, as for example, Brazil, Cuba, Chile and Colombia, and American enterprises in many of the Latin American countries have done substantially well.

On the other hand, the war has now made all of our investments in Europe and European possessions of dubious value.

The business of lending extravagantly and then gradually by processes of loss reducing the burden to manageable dimensions is not to be recommended. It is hardly more satisfactory to the borrower than to the lender. A better proportioned position had been emerging. In this field also—had the war not come—it may be surmised that the rough interplay of human interests, wills and decisions would not have resulted in too unfair or unsatisfactory an outcome.

Lastly, but of great importance, the course of gold movements between ourselves and the outside world during the past few years must be noted. These gold movements have been of enormous dimensions. In 1939 and so far in 1940 to take the extreme instance, our importations of gold were greater than our importations of all other goods. In short, despite the trend toward adjustment in our commercial and debt relations, gold shipment to us remained a primary form of payment. It would have been wiser to have acquired more of other goods, and less of gold. Further, the liquid assets of the world were transferred here—where they were thought to be out of the range of the conqueror, if not of the tax collector.

Only a short while ago, the gradual concentration of so large a part of the world's gold in the United States did not appear to have so serious an aspect, for much of it, as much as 6 or 7 billions of it, appeared to be here only for safekeeping. We had become the land of refuge not only for human beings but for liquid wealth. Our securities were acquired by foreigners. They built up balances in American banks. Given a stable and peaceful world, the movement might have been expected to reverse itself and the gold largely distribute itself. The war greatly lessens that possibility. Governments are selling many of the American securities and using up the balances.

If events continue thus, almost all of the gold that is in the United States will become irrevocably ours—and more may still come. It is impossible at this moment of writing to appraise the future possible usefulness of this vast hoard. My own anticipation is that if even a moderate measure of trust between nations is restored, gold will retain its general acceptability. But even though this should come about, we should possess far more of it than we shall need for any use or purpose now clearly perceivable. The great excess was expelled to us from the creditor countries of Western Europe by the weight of war. With it they sought to buy strength and safety. The black cloth of tragedy is draped over these golden bars. It may be that it will be given to us to use them again to lessen the suffering of a future time. And if that time is good to us, then, perhaps, the adjustment between ourselves and the outside world may be brought to wiser balance.

HOW AMERICAN POLICY WAS UNIQUE

Such were the problems which until recently filled our horizon. They were of sufficient gravity to force us to adopt some new and controversial measures. But they did not appear to call for any such immense revolution in international economic policies as most governments experienced.

Our methods of trading were not fundamentally modified. Resort was not had, in any serious measure, to new types of trade restrictions. International monetary operations between the United States and other countries, and capital movements between the United

States and other countries were left comparatively free. Americans were free to conduct exchanges of currencies—dollars for foreign currencies and foreign currencies for dollars—in much the same way as throughout American history. They were similarly free to engage in security dealings across national frontiers —as far as American law and governmental supervision were concerned.[1]

In avoiding great changes in these matters the country avoided also the marked modifications in the relation between private interests and the government such as took place in many other countries. American producers and merchants continued to look primarily to their own private activities in the conduct of their foreign business, and the government checks and regulations under which these activities go on were comparatively limited. Except as regards a few commodities, the export of which the American Government in 1939 definitely began to discourage (I have reference to the strategic materials of which we are deficient in supply and to those exports listed in the "moral embargo," and the conditions set forth in our neutrality legislation), they did not have to consult the government in regard to what might be sold abroad or to whom. So also Americans importing foreign goods, either for their own consumption or for use in production, have not had to seek their government's permission; they had to reckon merely with the same type of tariff protection which this country has always maintained. This was in com-

[1] The restrictions, by law and administrative order, upon the gold and other liquid assets in this country of Norway, Denmark, the Netherlands, Belgium and Luxemburg, and France, arose from special war situations and had special protective purposes.

plete contrast with the situation that came to rule in many other countries.

We retained virtually all our private commercial liberties in our relations with other countries. Beginning in 1934 we assumed leadership in the effort to preserve an operative international economic and financial system and mechanism. We undertook to hold before other countries by our actual practice, the idea of striving to maintain such a system, and of re-establishing the test of economic welfare as the guiding purpose of international economic relations.

Weighing our favorable circumstance during this period, the country inclined to the belief that our national life might be lived as though in a sunny garden, shut off from disorder and danger outside. The clouds darkened gradually and distantly over other lands; but few foresaw the fury and agony of storm they held; and the country, struggling with internal problems, was more open to comforting evasion than to proposals for action. But now all have become aware of the clouds over the sun, the gaps in the wall, the possible intruder in the garden. We have grown intensely aware of the importance of events outside. We live next to the radio. We walk our garden moodily, wondering what our future dangers and responsibilities may, or must be. All policies are under a newly intent scrutiny. Swift and decisive changes may be required.

V

OF OPULENCE AND DEFENSE

This final section is conceived and concluded in uncertainty.

Since September, 1939, Western and Central Europe have been a tragic battleground, Czechoslovakia and Poland have been divided and submerged. The thriving small Scandinavian states have been occupied or surrounded by German armies and shut off from the rest of the world. The invasion of Belgium and the Netherlands brought to an end their commercial and financial intercourse with the overseas world, leaving great colonies to conduct their trade independently and disconnectedly. France laid down its arms under the storm of fire and steel; most of the country is under German and Italian occupation; its economic intercourse with overseas countries and with the French colonies is disorganized and interrupted. The boundaries of Soviet Russia have been extended westward. The vast British Empire, itself a great international economic system, remains engaged in mortal struggle against Germany and Italy.

In the war area, and in regions closely attached to or connected with it, ordinary peacetime economic relations are virtually at an end. Within the countries at war the workers who have not been mobilized for military service are engaged in production for war needs, under governmental regulation of labor recruiting, transfer, hours and wages. Within the countries that have been invaded and conquered, millions of persons have been scattered by the armies that overwhelmed them, while the rest work amidst misery and uncertainty. A dark curtain has fallen over their lives; we cannot see through the drapes.

Ministries of trade, of finance, and of social economics have yielded place to ministries of economic warfare. Germany has reached out through every state on the European continent, with every device of force and diplomacy, to secure its war requirements. Italy, before its entry into the war, drew upon its already depleted reserves of gold and foreign exchange to buy the supplies it desired for its own assault. Great Britain, its fighting ships distributed over all the seas, has established a blockade of almost all the European continent. The progress of German arms has forced Britain to cast away calculations of caution in regard to conserving its resources and to buy or contract abroad with the utmost urgency everything that might help the beleaguered island to defend itself. After Italy's entry into the war and the collapse of France, the Mediterranean was closed and trade between the British Empire and almost all the continent ceased. The long voyage around the Cape and the convoys of gray ships across the Atlantic became the only trade routes left to supply the fighting British Empire.

The war has become a terrible autumn struggle. In these long and moon-lit September nights, Europe's economic saving and inheritance are being consumed in smoke and in the smoke are wrapped the bodies of fighting men.

Germany, already half-exultant in the thought of ultimate triumph, is expounding with arrogant dogma plans whereunder all of Europe, save possibly Russia, is to be put to work again under its unifying direction or control. If Germany should succeed in gaining final and quick victory, the still available supplies of food and materials, the still standing towns and factories, and the still operating means of transport would enable her to impose sufficient order and to requisition sufficient production to meet German needs amply— even though the occupied lands, especially Great Britain, would suffer a prolonged period of misery and depopulation. But if British resistance remains firm through the coming months and is sustained through the winter ahead, then all the continent will face deprivation and need. Factories will be increasingly destroyed. Means of transport, railways, docks and harbors will be increasingly torn asunder. Supplies of materials, of fuel and of foodstuffs will run low. Everything on the continent of Europe will be strained to sustain the war effort. Then even conquerors' plans may turn to dust.

No dry summary recital such as this, nor even the great black headlines of each day's newspaper, can bring true or complete comprehension of what has taken place. The mind and spirit can piece together and absorb fragments, such as the daily reported activities of governments, the sparse details of military communiqués, the many accounts of individual suffering, courage, terror, or oppression. But the interpretation and appraisal of the total of the vast change that is

of war. The trade with the countries now under German occupation had been largely a trade in peacetime staples, and the loss of this trade has further shifted the balance.

These developments in our trade relations have been affected in some degree by our neutrality legislation. It is probable that both our production and exportation of arms, ammunition, and implements of war were somewhat retarded and reduced by the provision in the original Act, since repealed, which prohibited their sale to belligerents. The ban on credits has likewise had some restrictive effect; England and France have more carefully measured their external purchasing power than they would have otherwise. The provisions having to do with the movement of American shipping have probably affected our trade with neutrals more than that with the belligerents. It is impossible precisely to measure these consequences; all that can be said with assurance is that our export trade has been *somewhat* less than it would have been if this legislation had not been on our statute books, and the military supplies available to France and England somewhat less.

CHANGES IN OUR INTERNAL ECONOMIC STRUCTURE

The wrench of war is plainly affecting our internal economic situation. Actual and potential surpluses within the country of some commodities, such as tobacco and cotton and corn, are greater than they would have been, while actual and potential demands for airplanes and ships, for steel and steel products, for chemicals having war use, for raw materials such as copper and the metallic alloys, have stimulated increased production and plant construction in these fields.

The difficult situation that might have faced producers of such commodities as tobacco and corn because of curtailed markets has been dealt with up to the present by governmental action; we have bought or made loans against the unmarketed surpluses. According to the way the future may go, these surpluses may remain a costly burden or may prove to serve an urgent need. Assisted by the government, the producing groups concerned have accepted the unfavorable impact of the war with calm and patience. The general upward economic movement within the country, and the strong underlying current of sympathy with Great Britain and France, have tended to foster this attitude.

It was inevitable that a war of this dimension and significance should bring changes in our internal economic structure. The course of the war has retarded or depressed some branches of production and trade and has stimulated others. Industry in general has been on guard against new undertakings that could not sustain themselves after the war crisis passed. But the assumption in recent months, especially by France and Great Britain, of the costs of plant expansion, and now and prospectively the even greater demands of our own defense program, will undoubtedly mean sizable shifts in working population and sizable industrial expansion that will not be required for these purposes if international trust and order should be restored. No matter what our form of economic organization, the execution of the desire to have our production remain available to France and Great Britain, and now in increasing ratio and extent the fulfillment of our defense program, would bring about a situation of this kind. In fact, any economic system that lacked the necessary flexibility to make such shifts would be a failure.

How far-reaching the economic shift may be, how long it may have to be continued, and what its issue may be—of these things no person can be certain. The purposes that are being served have priority. Compatible with these purposes it is possible and desirable, however, to take thought to the end that future readjustments may be as small as possible. Such precautionary effort would concern itself with keeping movements of working population within the limits actually required, with so arranging the financing of expansion that subsequent losses will be foreseen, and with preventing undue increases of prices and income. Up to the present both governmental policy and industrial and business judgment have shown themselves alert to these considerations.

No matter how successful such efforts may be, however, at some future time a new realignment of productive activity will become necessary. Thought, therefore, is required as to the means and measures which will make the new realignment as easy and satisfactory as possible. An extended social security system which will enable the individual to meet the hazards of future change will be an aid in carrying through the transition. In the monetary and banking sphere also, it may be suspected, new steps and measures will be required. The country is not likely to reconcile itself to the conclusion that full employment for all and the full use of our resources is only possible when conditions of war or needs of defense make it possible. It will not be content to see again either a return of the sharp crisis of

1921 and 1922 that came after the last war or the widespread unemployment and depression that prevailed during most of the last decade. We have the task of making our whole economic system work better.

Ability to achieve by free initiative and voluntary cooperation the productivity and strength we need—in rivalry with systems governed by compulsion—and ability to improve our economic life, these are the great tests of both our political and economic system that lie ahead. If we lack foresight, vitality, and national unity we shall know great turmoil.

DIGRESSION ON THE DEFENSE PROGRAM

The awakening of the United States to the possibility that the security and order of this country and other countries of this hemisphere might be in danger has brought us to undertake a vast new defense program. This may substantially affect our trade relations.

We are engaging, on the one hand, in the large-scale purchase of certain materials, vitally necessary in a war emergency, of which our stocks and our domestic production are inadequate. It is thereby planned to establish reserve stocks in addition to such ordinary commercial stocks as may be within the country. This will somewhat increase the import movement into this country during the rest of the year and perhaps for a longer period.

On the other hand, the requirements of the defense program have made it advisable to put under license the exportation of certain raw materials and manufactured products urgently required for the defense program. The list of exports so restricted includes arms, ammunition and implements of war, certain raw materials such as tin and rubber in which we are dependent on foreign sources of supply, certain other materials such as toluol and other chemicals for which our own need will expand greatly, and certain types of machine tools, produced only in limited quantity in this country and needed to manufacture armaments.

The needs of defense have been recognized to be paramount over all ordinary economic considerations, and as long as this period of danger and uncertainty may last, they must remain so. The defense effort, if I may digress for a moment, was tardily begun. Only as country after country fell helpless under the swift attack of tank and plane, have the American people become aware that attack might reach them and informed of the immensity of preparation and effort that defense requires. Illusion after illusion in which we had carelessly lived has now faded from the minds of all save those few who have so completely identified themselves with the illusions that they cannot change. We know now that the distribution of territorial, military and economic power in the outside world is of direct importance to us. We know that a most comprehensive and carefully measured technique has been devised for disrupting countries that, like the United States, permit differences of view and freedom of opinion, and which rely for decision and action upon the slow-moving processes of democracy. We know that any undermining of our unity can gravely hinder and retard the execution of defense effort. We know that the new instruments of war make it possible for a superior force to invade this hemisphere, to work destruction upon, and if preponderant enough even, in stages, to conquer it. We know that the successful defense of our land and liberties and of other parts of this hemisphere will require energy, patriotism, and cooperation. Laments over the divisions, the waste of time, the inertia, the partisanship by which France and Great Britain suffered are useless, save as they rouse and protect us from the same faults.

As part of our effort, our economic dealings with the rest of the world, in whole and in detail, will come under scrutiny in their bearing upon our ability to defend ourselves.

OUR MONETARY AND FINANCIAL RELATIONS IN WARTIME

In our monetary and financial relations we are dealing with a world in which government control has now become almost universal; these activities have no vitality except such as governments impart to them. Warring governments, struggling peoples and disturbed neutrals have sent their assets here for safety or for use. More and more both the ordinary and the extraordinary financial transactions of the world have centered here, the one country in which assets might be secure, and the one country from which goods can be procured and shipped without too much risk of interruption. Outside of the enormous territories within the German control, the mark today has little practical use. The franc ceased to be an international currency as the German armies advanced. The pound sterling, now under rigid control, has become only the unit of a fighting British Empire. Only the dollar remains in international use.

Up to the present at any rate the necessity or advantage of imposing complete control upon our own monetary exchanges with the rest of the world has not been clearly shown. But we have assumed guardianship over the assets here of the governments and peoples of countries that have suffered by invasion—of the Netherlands, of Denmark, of Belgium and Luxemburg, of Norway, and of France. This action was not dictated primarily by economic considerations. These assets had been attracted here by the hope that here they would be safe against seizure by a conquering force. The action taken was an attempt to give fulfillment to this purpose. Where the owners of these assets are in a position freely, themselves, to use them, permission to do so is given. To the extent that the owner of these assets may permanently lose effective power to claim and use them, a question of ultimate disposition may present itself; and in that case the question of protecting American interests and obligations may well claim recognition. But this is a matter on which guidance and decision lie in the actual development of events.

The enormous flow of gold and of liquid funds to this country has been accelerated by every German thrust. To what future use this store of gold may ultimately be directed is one that can be determined only as the conditions of the future are revealed. With skill and with wisdom it should prove most useful in the tasks of defense, of commerce, or of reconstruction— or of all three. To fail to put it effectively to these uses would be a great national blunder.

THE TURN IN OUR TRADE RELATIONS WITH THE OTHER AMERICAN REPUBLICS

The shifts and interruptions in our commerce have been less substantial and more easily managed than those experienced by some of the American Republics

—117—

—especially those whose trade losses have not been compensated by new war demands. Such countries as Argentina, Uruguay, Chile and Peru have always looked to continental European markets to buy a large part of those staple raw materials which are their main exports. As the war has advanced, the effects of this interruption of trade have been cumulatively felt by those countries.

The decline has been irregular. For various minerals, for example, war demand has actually increased income received by producers and exporters. But here and there the loss has been abrupt, as in the case of corn, nitrates, and coffee. The decline of income suffered in some of the Republics, if it were to continue, would mean widespread depression and loss and a grave weakness in the public finances.

Because of the simple economic basis of the life of most of these American nations and the ample supply of the necessities which most of them possess, the type of difficulty they may face is in a sense less serious than that arising in a more highly organized economic system, like our own. But it would be serious enough to affect the fortunes of many and to destroy the hope with which these countries live.

During the war period the dependence of these countries upon the United States as a market for their products and as a source of emergency assistance has increased. Our purchases of their products have been well sustained. In the nine months from September, 1939 through May, 1940 our imports from the twenty Latin-American Republics amounted to 460 million dollars as compared with 352 million dollars for the same months a year earlier. The rise in economic activity within the

United States under the spur of the defense program forecasts still further increase.

Currently both national and hemispheric arrangements of new and extended character have been brought forward for consideration both here and in the other American states. The most satisfactory basis for permanently strengthened economic relations between the United States and the other American states lies in the reciprocal enlargement of the commerce between them. Some of their primary products, such as coffee, tin, bananas, cacao and carpet wool, now enjoy favorable treatment under the United States tariff. Many of the others are subject only to tariffs of moderate character, for example, hides and skins, and petroleum. But some —of which we ourselves produce or might produce surpluses beyond our own needs, such as wheat, meats, and flaxseed—are shut out of our market or are restricted by high duties. The current trade disturbance brings again clearly to attention the question of whether we might not, after suitable negotiation, lessen some of our present restrictions. Such action of course should be weighed in the terms of the long-run or permanent relationship. If the outcome of the war makes it wise and imperative that every possible economic bond be established between the American states, the necessary measures, whatever they might be, should be taken. Possible tariff reductions, or even preferential tariffs, and commodity agreements for joint control of production and marketing are among the possible measures that present themselves for consideration.

The field of cooperation in commodity production and marketing, in particular, offers various and flexible possibilities. Such commodity agreements might be worked out one by one or might stem from some general and more comprehensive agreement elaborated between the American Republics. If their application should cause sudden and substantial loss or displacement to producers within this country, suitable safeguards or compensation will be required for those bearing the loss.

We should also keep under constant review in the light of events whether the present form of our trade agreements and the present powers of the Executive with respect to foreign trade show themselves to be adequate. It may be that it will be necessary in some instances—to offset the pressure of others or to protect our own interest—to resort to modified forms of agreement and to place enlarged powers in the hands of the Executive comprehensively to control imports, exports, or payments between ourselves and others.

Should necessity dictate, neither novelty of method nor preconceived notion, nor unusual difficulties of administration, nor large initial expense should be permitted to defeat the purpose. The events that have been changing the world have moved with lightning speed. This is not the best pace at which to develop new working economic institutions. But we must prove equally capable of speed if it is required. It is impossible to know how far in any or all directions it may be wise and feasible to go. Each morning, in this war world, judgment must shape itself anew, as the task defines itself, ready to meet new situations.

Whether we are dealing merely with a crisis that will pass or with a more prolonged period of difficulty, the United States is in a position to grant financial assistance to others. To meet problems created by falling revenues and decreased proceeds from exports, many of these countries have received from the American Government emergency support in the form of loans. This help has been in moderate amounts but readily extended. Among the countries receiving such support are Argentina, Chile, Colombia, Ecuador, and Peru.

The loans have been of genuine aid in providing the means of offsetting unemployment and loss and in making it possible to buy goods deemed important for development. Continuation of this type of financing, where sought and after careful examination and judgment in each instance, is well advised.

However, as far as it may be possible, effort should be made to avoid augmentation of the debt burden of the other countries. Increased purchases by us and others will provide needed income without adding to that burden. Such is the justification for expenditure for purchases of surpluses of other countries which we would not buy in ordinary course. Under the one method the risk involved is that the debt burden will prove to be beyond the reasonable ability of the borrowing countries to repay. Under the other the risk would be that these surpluses will never find a market or a use that will repay the outlay. Here again wise action must be guided by the desires and ideas of the other American nations and by the possibilities of finding a strong basis for genuine cooperation.

In supporting these economic and financial measures I would not wish to appear to have fallen into the belief that merely by providing an improved or assured market for the products of the other American nations, or by financial assistance can the economic advancement, security or cooperation of the American nations be assured. That would be a superficial optimism.

It is essential, if these ends are to be assured, that economic cooperation have its counterpart in a conjunction of diplomatic and political policy. This can come about only if each and all give devoted support to the maintenance of the independence and security of the American nations. And finally, the United States must prove that it has the military strength strong enough to protect this country, and if need be, other American countries against attacks or subordination. Our leadership must rest on our strength, not upon our need. In this contemporary world the cooperation of the weak is spurned.

What economic course may be necessary or best for the American nations to pursue in the future is still somewhat uncertain. No matter what the coming months may unfold, it is clear that it would be to the potential advantage of all to broaden their economic and financial relationships. But the extent of action that may be urgently required, whether a firm enough basis exists to build upon, and whether effort will have to be devoted largely to the purposes of maintaining security rather than of directly serving economic welfare, still cannot be conclusively foretold. The great decisions in this field, as in all others, lie ahead. With stimulated minds, energy, and resolution we must face them.

What is done by each country, how it is done, and in what spirit it is done—all will be important in determining the outcome. The measures taken by each must be sufficient, they must be feasible, they must be reciprocal, and they must fit the pattern of relations with countries outside this hemisphere. They must be, as far as possible, worked out by common accord.

THE NIGHT-PUZZLING FUTURE

Difficult as it may be to try to discern the character of the economic relationships among the American nations, and the direction of the economic policies and institutions that may be required, it is still more difficult to foretell what international economic relationships may prevail elsewhere and what the part of the United States in them will be. That must be in the nature of night-puzzling and restless conjecture until out of the blood of battle and spirit of nations the lines of the world's political future are determined.

The whole account of international economic relations that has been set forth in the earlier sections of this analysis shows how inevitably they are shaped by the course of political and social change. We have seen that no matter how perfectly the skein of policy may be wound upon the bobbin, the upward and downward plunge of events, like the needle on the sewing machine, determines what happens to the thread.

Because of our wealth and our strength, whatever course of policy the United States may decide to follow will influence that of others. The nature of our policy and the firmness and skill shown in its application will to some extent determine what course other countries take. But clearly it would be unwise as well as ineffective to decide our policy except with constant reference to the conditions that prevail outside of the United States and the actions of other countries. Elementary considerations of national security and of economic welfare will both make essential accurate appreciation of outside events and swift adaptation to deal with them.

Consider the all-embracing uncertainties with which judgment must reckon. Until this war shall end and the future balance of forces reveal themselves, we do not know in what economic condition the world will be, nor what will be the character of the economic organization of many countries, nor what methods they will use in conducting their trade and finance with outside countries, nor whether internal social revolutions may follow the war, nor, finally, whether the powers that emerge dominant from the present struggle will work for international stability and order or use their diplomacy or force for contrary ends. Our decision and our policy must be responsive to the answer that the future may yield to each of these uncertainties. Thus it would be futile, at this time, to attempt to put forward conclusive judgment as regards the policies and methods that we should pursue, or to enter into minute or comprehensive detail. Hence, all that is possible is to suggest the general character of the policies that might be pursued and the relationships that might be sought according to whether the future wears one face or another.

It is clear that international economic relations of a fruitful and uninterrupted character can only operate in a world marked, both in belief and practice, by trust and order. Without these, creative and beneficial international economic effort will be greatly hindered. Trade and pillage, financial certainty and fright, industry and persecution cannot satisfactorily go on together. The productive interchange of goods and of capital between nations requires that they be committed to living at peace with each other, to the accordance of fair consideration to each other, and to the respect of rights and interests even of the weak.

If the future should so develop that the United States has no substantial cause to fear threatening attempts against its security and independence, the aims of economic welfare and general benefit that we have sustained in the past would remain valid and can be retained as dominant in our economic relations with other countries. The underlying economic structure of the United States would continue to counsel the effort to carry on a substantial trade with the rest of the world. The activity of business interests, encouraged by official disposition, would be exercised to restore world markets for main commodities. Our great reserves of gold and liquid capital would be available to respond to economic opportunity elsewhere. Our habits, our institutions and our general desire to sustain private enterprise would continue to incline us to leave the conduct of our international economic relations primarily to private interests—with the hope that experience should have given sufficient instruction to avoid the main errors of the past. If conditions should permit and justify such a line of policy, advantage would be yielded, not only to ourselves but to other countries. Our natural resources, our productive skill, our capital supplies, our technical knowledge would again become available to them.

But both this general type of policy and this method of conducting our economic relations will be inadequate to protect our national interests and security if we face a world in which force rules and danger faces us. Then our policy and methods will have to be concentrated on the task of building our own military strength; and far-reaching departures from the past in many respects will be required.

In that event, it is certain to influence increasingly our future economic and financial policies. The lines on the foot rule that in the past we have been accustomed to use were drawn to measure economic benefits and international trust. That foot rule will have to be placed in the foundation stone and laid aside for building anew when this era is over. Instead, the foot rule employed will have to be lined to measure degrees of national strength. With this new foot rule we should have to gauge afresh every aspect of our economic and financial relationships. We should have to select the economic methods that are most suitable and effective as instruments of power diplomacy. In respect to each of our exports we should have to ask: first, will possible defense needs enable us to spare them; second, will the country that is securing them prove to be a friend or a possible enemy; third, can we directly secure in return for them any commodity that will contribute to our military strength? In regard to our imports we should have to ask: first, do they contribute to our military strength; second, are we buying them in those places where we wish to encourage production; and, third, will the dollars that we may pay be used for a friendly or unfriendly purpose?

Such is the variety of questions that immediately intrudes itself into the making of commercial policy when a people must think primarily of safeguarding its territory and its independence. It is obvious that if we are compelled to give primary consideration to matters of this character, we should have to exercise more governmental control of our trade relations than we ever have in the past except in time of war. In such a world though our trade might be substantial, it would be uncertain and controlled. Our policy would be self-protective, guarded, nationalist, perhaps regional. This would be new in American life and foreign policy— were we forced to sustain it for a considerable period. We are not trained in such a use of our economic force nor are we disciplined for it, nor is it congenial to us. For these reasons it is probable that many foreign countries think we should never be able to follow this course effectively. The constraints that it would require in subordination and organization of private interests and the unity of decision within government— of all these things they have believed us incapable. That judgment we shall swiftly disprove.

The same set of considerations will play as well a decisive part in determining *what methods* we may follow in the conduct of our trade and financial operations.

Further, if after the war many important countries retain their present thoroughgoing control over their commerce and their exchanges, the question will present itself—on purely economic grounds—whether American interests can be adequately safeguarded without adopting in turn similar measures of control in regard to these countries. If many other governments retain control over every important export item, over every payment which they permit their citizens to make to Americans on commercial and debt account, and if they use such methods to the injury of American interests, or to force concessions from us, a readiness to resort to similar or equivalent methods on our part may be essential.

But any such necessity is apt to be far less if it is a world from which the danger of aggression passes, than if the contrary is the case.

Our times were shaped by busy, striving men. Probing scientific minds attained a vastly enlarged knowledge of the earth's physical and chemical elements and how to manipulate them. Invention applied itself to the making of new means of transport, communication, production and destruction. Business enterprise established these in daily life. Millions of workmen bent their backs and used their skill to operate the machines, pour the cement, build the towers, string the wires. Spurring on the effort was the need for earning a living or the wish to gain wealth or esteem. But most of those who droned in this workshop of the decades possessed as well the sense that their effort was serving some general good—that in sum and ultimate total it would improve the condition of men, lessen toil, check nature's perils and supplement its bounty.

Each time man shifted dirt, dug ore, overcame gravity, he shifted also his relation to his fellow men. Each road built, each hull laid, each flying field levelled, brought into closer exposure, in all aspects and hours of living, the various peoples, races and governments of the world. They became intimately connected in the political realm as were the small city-states on the peninsula of Greece about whose experience and destiny Plato, in the Republic, wrote the greatest of all political estimates.

The change in the earth's dimensions was taken by

the economists to forecast a drawing together of nations in peaceful cooperation. Once the spectre of incessant population growth was laid, economic reasoning put aside its "dismal air"; concerning the long and further prospect of human affairs a hopeful outlook began to emerge. The increased power to produce was counted upon to satisfy needs and soften the struggle for survival or subsistence. Science was counted upon to instruct, trade to distribute. A growing spirit of understanding and tolerance appeared to be entering human affairs. Minds released from bleak fears and doubts moved forward with exhilaration, and expressed it in their working effort.

We are now back again in the midst of grim chronicle. For the second time within a generation deep and destructive conflict has come. The extending international economic relations through which the world's productive effort was shared had been carried forward mainly by the capitalist, trading empires of Western Europe. Truly to repair the damage of the last war and to reform and improve their institutions and conditions of life, full fifty years were needed. Only twenty have been granted. Germany, Italy, Japan and Russia each in its own way has moved to acquire new territories by force of arms; and each has poured criticism or contempt upon the international economic relations that prevailed, and the ideals they served.

The delineation of the future of these relations must await the course and outcome of the present struggle. We do not know what air we shall breathe, what need there may be in our own country to devote main energies for our own defense, how best private and public activities should be combined to meet emerging circumstances, what realm for justice, what hope for enduring peace on which international economic life may be established.

Faith and effort, in this hour, must proceed without the benefit of prophecy. In those imbued with the pattern for which reason reached, faith will sustain itself, and from them effort will be forthcoming. For they had graven on their minds, despite deficiency and inelasticity of doctrine, a vision in which economic activity united the world into a society of independent and equal nations, serving both strong and weak.

BIBLIOGRAPHY

CHAPTER I

Ellsworth, P. T., *International Economics,* New York, 1938.
Eulenberg, Franz, article on "International Trade—Institutional Framework," in *Encyclopedia of the Social Sciences,* New York, 1931.
Haberler, Gottfried, *The Theory of International Trade,* New York, 1936.
Taussig, F. W., *International Trade,* New York, 1927.
———, *Principles of Economics,* 4th Edition, New York, 1939.

CHAPTER II

Chalmers, Henry, "Foreign Tariffs and Commercial Policies." Annual summaries appearing in U. S. Department of Commerce, *Commerce Reports.*
League of Nations, *World Economic Survey* (Annual volumes).
Rappard, William E., *Post-War Efforts for Freer Trade* (Geneva Economics Studies, Vol. IX, No. 2, March, 1938).
Tasca, H. J., *World Trading Systems,* Paris, 1939.
Tippetts, Charles S., *Autarchy: National Self-Sufficiency* (Public Policy Pamphlets, No. 5, University of Chicago Press, 1936).

CHAPTER III

Dietrich, Ethel B., *World Trade,* New York, 1939.
Heuser, Heinrich, *Control of International Trade,* London and Philadelphia, 1939.
League of Nations, *Enquiry into Clearing Agreements* (1935).
Snyder, Richard C., "The Most Favored National Clause and Recent Trade Practices," *Political Science Quarterly,* March, 1940, pp. 77-97.

CHAPTER IV

Beard, Charles A., *The Open Door at Home*, New York, 1934.

Committee of Inquiry into National Policy in International Economic Relations, *International Economic Relations* (1934), Minneapolis, 1934.

Extension of Reciprocal Trade Agreements Act, Hearings before the Committee on Ways and Means, Seventy-sixth Congress, Third Session on H. J. Res. 407. (January, 1940), Vol. I, pp. 4-15, 116-22, 713-45.

Feis, Herbert, "The Open Door at Home," *Foreign Affairs*, Vol. 13, pp. 600-11, July, 1935.

Gantenbein, James W., *Financial Question in United States Foreign Policy*, New York, 1939.

Gayer, Arthur D. and Schmidt, Carl T., *American Economic Foreign Policy* (American Coordinating Committee for International Studies, 1939).

Hull, Cordell, "The Foreign Commercial Policy of the United States," address before the Chamber of Commerce of the U. S., May 2, 1935 (Department of State publication No. 733).

Lewis, Cleona, *America's Stake in International Investments*, Washington, 1938.

Wallace, Henry A., *America Must Choose*, New York and Boston, 1934.

CHAPTER V

Bonn, Moritz J., "Planning for Peace," *American Economic Review*, Supplement March, 1940, pp. 272-80.

DeWilde, John C., "Germany's Controlled Economy," *Foreign Policy Reports*, Vol. XIV, No. 24, March 1, 1939.

Patterson, Ernest M., *The Economic Bases of Peace*, New York, 1939.

Poole, K. E., *German Financial Policies*, 1932-1939, Cambridge, 1939.

Trueblood, H. J., "War and United States-Latin American Trade," *Foreign Policy Reports*, Vol. XV, No. 18, Dec. 1, 1939.